D1545794

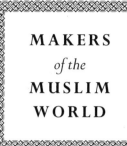

MAKERS
of the
MUSLIM
WORLD

Husain Ahmad Madani

SELECTION OF TITLES IN THE MAKERS OF THE MUSLIM WORLD SERIES

Series editor: Patricia Crone,
Institute for Advanced Study, Princeton

For current information and details of other books in the
series, please visit www.oneworld-publications.com

MAKERS
of the
MUSLIM
WORLD

Husain Ahmad Madani

The Jihad for Islam and India's Freedom

BARBARA D. METCALF

ONEWORLD
OXFORD

A Oneworld Book

Published by Oneworld Publications 2009

Copyright © Barbara D. Metcalf 2009

ISBN 978–1–85168–579–0

Typeset by Jayvee, Trivandrum, India
Printed and bound in India for Imprint Digital

Oneworld Publications
185 Banbury Road
Oxford OX2 7AR
England
www.oneworld-publications.com

CONTENTS

SOURCES AND ACKNOWLEDGEMENTS

Maulana Madani has provided any biographer with a substantial corpus of useful writings. Apart from some scholarly works, written in Arabic, most of his writings were in Urdu, including memoirs written during two of his periods of imprisonment, one from the early 1920s and one from World War II. These are key documents for reconstructing the first half of his life. He wrote pamphlets, short books, and newspaper articles; he also delivered many public addresses to organizations and meetings that were subsequently published. He conducted a vast correspondence, several volumes of which are available in print. Invaluable as well are accounts of his life by his contemporaries. Of the many helpful secondary sources I have used, I particularly want to acknowledge two excellent analyses of Madani's religious thought by Peter Hardy and Yohanan Friedmann (Hardy 1971; Friedmann 1971).

I also gratefully acknowledge the courtesies of those associated with the Nehru Memorial Museum and Library, the British Library, and the libraries of the University of California at Davis and the University of Michigan in helping me secure necessary materials. I owe special thanks to Mohammad Anwer Hussain of the Jamiat Ulama-i-Hind for his many kindnesses; to Katherine Prior, for assistance in securing British government documents; to Priya Satia, for her generosity in sharing with me notes she made for her important study of British policies in the Middle East during World War I; and to Sadia Saeed at Michigan, for her help in utilizing Madani's letters. Arshad Zaman generously secured for me published materials from Pakistan.

I have presented material about Maulana Madani at several venues, and am grateful to the organizers and participants at those events. I was especially honored to speak at a book launch (for Madani 2005) convened by Maulana Madani's grandson, Maulana Mahmood Madani, which was held at the India Habitat Centre, New Delhi, in December 2004. My grateful thanks also to Mushirul Hasan, at Jamia Millia Islamia; Deana Heath and Chandan Mathur, at Trinity College, Dublin; Crispin Bates, at the University of Edinburgh; David Bates, at the Anglo-American Conference at the University of London; Abigail McGowan, at the University of Virginia; Tithi Bhattacharya, at Purdue University; Rochana Majumdar, at the University of Chicago; and Mark Kenoyer, at the South Asia Conference at the University of Wisconsin. Two especially generous colleagues, David Gilmartin and Lee Schlesinger, provided comments on a draft of the entire manuscript; one could not ask for better critics or friends. Warm thanks as well to the anonymous reader for Oneworld for careful, detailed, and insightful comments. Finally, thanks to Azfar Moin for the maps; to Patricia Crone for inviting me to write the biography in the first place; and, as always, to my spouse, Thomas Metcalf, for his unfailing support.

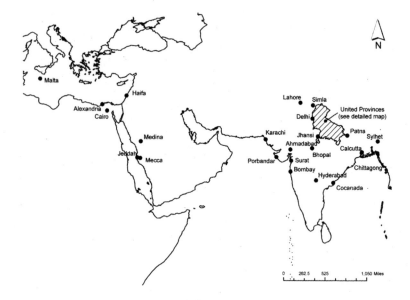

Places in India and beyond where Husain Ahmad Madani travelled.

Cities in the United Provinces mentioned in the text where Madani travelled or lived.

INTRODUCTION

This is a book about Maulana Husain Ahmad Madani (1879–1957), one of the most important Muslim figures in the history of twentieth-century South Asia. He was a traditionally educated Islamic scholar who studied at the Darul 'Ulum at Deoband, the *madrasa* that gives the "Deobandi" sectarian orientation its name. Maulana Madani served as the seminary's principal for the final three decades of his life. He was actively engaged in India's nationalist movement and joined the Gandhian non-cooperation movement at its inception, dressing in the handloomed cloth that was its symbol and urging others to do so as well. Beginning in 1916, Maulana Madani was arrested once a decade until India's Independence in 1947, spending over seven years in British detention.

As Indian independence approached in 1947, Maulana Madani stood as a staunch opponent of those calling for the establishment of a separate homeland for the Muslims of India. Instead, he wrote, argued, and campaigned for the position that Muslims could live as observant Muslims in a religiously plural society where they would be full citizens of an independent, secular India. His importance rests in his being both a political activist and an influential scholar who made Islamic arguments to support his position. Maulana Madani's life and thought thus challenge common assumptions about the incompatibility between Islam and democracy. More fundamentally, his life serves as an example of the varied and creative ways in which traditionalist Islamic scholars can engage with their scholarly tradition to address the political and social issues of their day.

As a traditionalist scholar (that is, one of the *'ulama*), Maulana Madani focused his life on mastering, interpreting, and transmitting sacred texts and writings about them, in his case within the Sunni, Hanafi tradition. Contrary to popular stereotypes, including those

1

articulated by modernist contemporaries who opposed his position, scholars like Madani did not make their arguments in a vacuum. Though he articulated his positions as a religious scholar, the context for Madani's Islamic arguments in favor of a shared Indian nationhood rested on his engagement with many dimensions of public life. Like other leaders of the nationalist movement, the Indian National Congress, he insisted on the exploitative nature of colonialism and the self-interested motivations that lay behind many colonial policies. At the end of the colonial period, he firmly believed that the British were encouraging the country's partition in order to weaken the independent state and allow for continued intervention. He insisted that the fundamental institution of contemporary political life was the territorial nation state and that the political culture of the day was one of citizen-based civic and human rights. He held rival visions of organizing a polity on Islamic grounds to be unrealistic.

Madani's contextually based and informed arguments counter the widespread but erroneous tendency to discount Islamically articulated arguments as products of narrow textual analysis. This predisposition to define Muslims almost exclusively in terms of their putative static "religion" has a long heritage. In the Indian context, it is rooted in colonial categories of analysis. Such categories fostered the view that the problems faced by Muslims were peculiar to them and derived from Islam. It meant that only Muslims could represent Muslims. And as colonial "sociology" came to be embedded in a range of institutional arrangements, Muslims and others of necessity identified themselves as such. Although Maulana Madani was a product of this culture, he challenged significant dimensions of it, not least what he saw as an attempt to encourage Hindu–Muslim difference in order to divert attention from the economic exploitation that colonialism had brought that affected all Indians. His opposition to the British was grounded in such concerns and not, for example, in "religious" opposition to the British rulers as Christian. In the same way, his opposition to the Pakistan movement did not simply derive from "religious" antagonism to the leadership of non-observant Muslims like Muhammad Ali Jinnah (1876–1948).

Recently, the scholar Mahmood Mamdani has argued that far too much western analysis of contemporary political activities on the part of Muslims assumes that their only political motivation is "religious," and thus the only distinction among Muslims is that between "moderates," who represent "good" interpretations of Islamic texts, and extremists, shaped by "bad." This culturalist line of argumentation, he has pointed out, occludes fundamental geo-political contexts that have shaped Muslim behavior, specifically, in the cases he analyzes, Cold War and other interventions in Africa (Mamdani 2004). Similarly, the French sociologist Olivier Roy insists that arguments about political Islam in Europe go astray when they emphasize continuities from the Qur'an instead of socio-political issues that have also produced modern European radical-ism, contemporary Christian movements, and so forth (Roy 1998). In short, one is on firmer ground assuming that what matters to Muslims is the whole range of social, political, economic, and cul-tural interests that matter to everyone else.

The biography below opens with an account of Maulana Madani's arrest in Mecca in 1915 and his subsequent internment on Malta (Chapters 1 and 2). These events marked the turning point of his life. An account of his formative years of education and teaching follows (Chapter 3). Chapter 4 picks up the story of Maulana Madani's departure from Malta and his return to India in 1920. Maulana Madani was immediately catapulted into public life. As his writings and speeches from those days make clear, he accepted the fundamen-tal categories of the "nation," and he also in fact accepted the colonial categories of presumed homogeneous, census-based "religious com-munities" of Hindus and Muslims. In the Jamiat Ulama-i-Hind (the Organization of Indian Ulama), the Congress, and other organiza-tions, he participated in the democratic processes of the "civil soci-ety" institutions of his day, and, with his colleagues, he grappled with issues of representation and federalism in envisioning the future state. He challenged colonial policies in terms of Britain's own offi-cial values, asserting rights of self-determination, non-interference in religion, international law, human rights, and, of special importance to India's Muslims, the cultural rights of linguistic, religious, and other minorities. The assumption that a scholar like him was motivated by some hermetic "Islam" is thus misplaced.

Maulana Madani entered Indian politics through the Khilafat Movement, the post-World War I defense of the role of the Ottoman sultan as "caliph," ruler of a heterogeneous domain, and protector of the Holy Cities of the Arabian Hijaz. One might easily conclude that this cause, if any, was "religious," even irrational. It certainly was "Muslim," taken up by minority Muslim Indians who thus enhanced their own importance through transnational ties. But for Maulana Madani the cause was fundamentally stimulated by colonial politics that concerned other Indians too, namely, the politics of failed promises and maneuverings to extend, not withdraw, European power. Maulana Madani, based in Medina, had witnessed the British role in Arabian affairs during World War I at first hand. Similarly, Maulana Madani's opposition to British colonialism in India consistently focused on specific grievances of colonial injustice. He later would oppose Pakistan, first and foremost, because he believed that two countries, instead of one strong united one, would afford opportunities for continued European intervention and meddling (as Cold War politics for decades in fact confirmed). He presciently regarded the idea of dividing the Muslim population as utterly unrealistic, given the social and economic relationships of Hindus and Muslims throughout the country, even in the Muslim-majority areas (Chapter 6).

But most importantly, Maulana Madani opposed Pakistan as someone deeply committed to a Muslim presence in the whole of India. He couched his argument within the framework of modern territorial nationalism, asserting Muslim indigeneity and ties to the land. He thus challenged Hindu "communalists," who marginalized non-Hindus in their vision of Indian nationalism. In this, he also broke with Muslim separatists ready to sever their tie to the larger territory. In taking this position, he, like other Indians, moved beyond historic patterns of de-territorialized loyalties in favor of the modern commitment to national belonging defined by homeland.

Maulana Madani argued that India had had an Islamic presence from the beginning of human history; that the blessed soil of India was the repository of centuries of deceased holy men; and that India was Muslim Indians' only and beloved home. To those who attacked him as a "slave" of Hindus who sacrificed the interests of Islam, he replied that he in fact saw Islam's true interest. Only by remaining within India could Muslims fulfill their obligation continuously to present the message of Islam to others, a classic argument now presented within a nationalist discourse. Far from seeing Pakistan as ushering in an Islamic utopia, he joined others in the Congress in dismissing its aristocratic and "feudal" leadership as reactionary in contrast to the progressive (*taraqqi pasand*) orientation of the nationalists.

As David Gilmartin has recently argued, the historic pattern of Muslim societies was one in which the *'ulama* engaged little with the realities of actual state power (Gilmartin 2005: 54). This pattern gained even more vitality during the period of colonial rule when the gulf between state and society was even more profound. The moral community existed apart from the state. The bonds of loyalty and identity tying modern citizens to homelands appear antithetical to this earlier model, and, as Peter Hardy has astutely noted, many statements of the Jamiat Ulama-i-Hind, even as it joined Hindus in the anti-colonial struggle, in fact paid scant attention to territorial loyalties and rather espoused a confederation of communities, unlinked to land as such. Maulana Madani's contribution to the political thought of the *'ulama*, Hardy suggests, was, in fact, to foster the innovative concept of territorial nationalism in which the new state would protect the cultural autonomy of religious groups (Hardy 1971: 37).

Maulana Madani's sense of loyalty to a specific territory was shaped, one might suggest, by his relentless concern with British economic exploitation. The historian Manu Goswami (2004) has argued that there were two central themes in Indian nationalist thought. One was colonial exploitation, shading into "autarkic" economic theories that wanted to preserve India's wealth within borders that were sharply defined and imagined in the course of colonial rule. Those borders were made real by the coverage of nationally focused newspapers, of which Madani was an active reader (Abu Salman Shahjahanpuri 2002), and by such experience as train travel, again a familiar part of his life from the time of his first childhood trip to distant Chittagong. The second nationalist theme, Goswami argues, was an "organic" one that made the land of India a veritable living being, shading into the powerful nationalist metaphor of India as a goddess, "Mother India," who was regularly addressed in nationalist settings with the song in her honor, "Bande Mataram." Maulana Madani was seemingly untroubled by the Hindu theme implicit in this imagery, which some Muslims urgently protested. Madani did not himself take up such images, but seems to have been interested in attempts to interpret these images metaphorically (Abu Salman Shahjahanpuri 2002: I, 295–296). Moreover, given the cultural pluralism he espoused, perhaps since he himself put forth Islamic myths for Indian nationalism, there was room for Hindus to think of India as they too saw fit.

Madani interacted with a range of Muslim leaders who challenged his position in the interwar years. Among them, the best known was the great poet and proponent of Muslim territorial autonomy, Muhammad Iqbal (1877–1938) (Chapter 5). The debate gave Maulana Madani an opportunity to display his traditionalist scholarship in support of his commitment to "composite nationalism." Readers may be surprised to see the extent to which Islamic scholars used their mastery of classic forms of analysis and argumentation in order to address specific historic and political contexts. India in the colonial period had seen a revitalization of scholarly Islamic traditions as opposed to blindly imitating them as the stereotyped image has it. The high standard of Islamic scholarship in India during this period is evident in the fact that Maulana Madani, trained at Deoband, was able to establish himself in his early years as a distinguished teacher to an international audience in the holy city of Medina itself.

Maulana Madani at once participated in the colonial and

transnational discourses of his day as well as in a rich and complex Islamic tradition that gave his political positions legitimacy and, reciprocally, made the tradition relevant. There was much more to his life, however, than his political thought and actions alone, above all his profound engagement in the traditional institutions and practices of Sufism. He was widely revered for the depth and extent of the disciplines and bonds of discipleship that he cultivated. Of the many biographies written about Maulana Madani, the Deoband website recommends one whose title is *Anfas qudsiyya* (A Breath of Saintliness). The author's goal, he tells us, is not to write from a historical, political, or philosophical point of view but rather from a *tablighi* vantage, which we can take to mean an attempt to show Maulana Madani as a living embodiment of Islamic truths offered for the reader's response ('Azizu'r-Rahman 1958: 17). Similarly a Pakistani volume includes testimonials to Maulana Madani's "personality" (*shakhsiyat*), among them one by Maulana Sami'ul Haqq, known today for his role in educating the Taliban, whose politics could not, of course, differ more dramatically from Madani's (Bukhari 1972: 217–220). For his followers, Maulana Madani was judged selfless, learned, faithful, devoted to his elders, and attentive to his followers. And he was viewed as someone close to God whose life was graced with divine dreams and miracles.

In his political life, however, Maulana Madani encountered other prevalent images, many still current, of what it meant to be a traditionalist scholar or even simply a Muslim. In arresting him in 1916, for example, the colonial rulers made the undue assumption, noted above, that whatever Muslims did could be explained by "Islam" – its supposed fanaticism, its intransigence – to the exclusion of political, economic, and human rights grievances, as excerpts from their interrogation notes show (Chapter 2). That an arrest and prolonged detention like Maulana Madani's may sow the seeds of the kind of opposition the ruling power hopes to defeat is, of course, another dimension of the story that re-echoes today. Negative stereotypes may also mean that fellow politicians marginalize the role of traditionalist Muslims. In the Indian nationalist movement, neither colonial officials nor Indian nationalist leaders accorded much importance to the views of the Muslim religious leadership in the final deliberations that led to Independence and Partition. Both colonial officials and many westernized Indians marked the Islamic scholars as simply "religious" or as speakers of only the vernacular, intellectually "backward." This pejorative image of Islamic leaders within South Asia did not end with Partition.

One could tell Maulana Madani's story as one of a heroic, but ultimately failed, battle. The Partition, after all, did take place, and it happened at enormous and enduring cost (Chapter 6). Although one recent biographer ranks Maulana Madani's importance with Nehru and Gandhi (Goyal 2004), he is in fact today little known. His Indian admirers, however, above all those who follow his sectarian Deobandi orientation and belong to the Jamiat Ulama-i-Hind, claim him as an inspiring example of a "freedom fighter" who faced multiple incarcerations, campaigned for a united India, and stood for the creation of a secular state. Recent publications, like the biography just noted, have sought to make Maulana Madani a focus of Indian pride in the wake of anti-Muslim rhetoric and violence that has challenged the very presence of Muslims in India.

Wilfred Cantwell Smith, a pioneer scholar of "Modern Islam in India" (the title of his 1945 book), pointed to the importance of Indian Muslims in confronting the issues posed by religious pluralism, a problem, he argued, that would confront all Muslims – and, one might add, all religious thinkers – in an ever more integrated world. Maulana Madani stands as an example of someone who faced this issue. Devastated as he was by Partition, Maulana Madani's own response in 1947 was to rejoice at the end of colonialism and to summon Muslims in a free India to faithful citizenship and Islamic practice.

This short study only begins to tell the story of a life that deserves renewed attention in the history of political activities in the final decades of British rule in India. It is a story of the intellectually and spiritually abundant life of a traditionalist scholar, rich in relationships of loyalty and responsibility to kinfolk, spiritual mentors, and scholarly teachers, as well as to countless people to whom he offered leadership and help. It is a story as well of a scholar and activist who made creative responses to the worldly issues of his day – colonialism, nationalism, economic exploitation, minority rights – from within the historic Islamic tradition. Not only Maulana Madani's particular life, but the *kind* of life he represents, is one that well merits retelling, especially at a time like the present when uninformed stereotypes about Muslims and Islamic politics are so strong.

* * *

What was our subject's name? The custom of a "family name" in India as elsewhere became standard only in recent times. "Husain Ahmad" was our subject's given name, and I use that name in his early years. He also from birth had the name "Chiragh-i Muhammad," the Light of Muhammad. This was his "date name," devised so that the Arabic letters, each the equivalent of a number, added up to the date of his birth. At one point he was signing his letters from prison with this name, and it was sometimes used by his followers because of the honor it conveyed. Once Husain Ahmad had studied at Deoband and began teaching, he was accorded the title of "Maulana," a recognition that he was a scholar of Islam. Many people also added to his name the title "Saiyyid," indicating putative genealogical descent from the Prophet Muhammad. In Medina, where he lived for roughly a decade and a half as a young man, he was known as "Maulana Hindi," the scholar from India; reciprocally in India he was accorded the locative "Madani," to indicate his ties to Medina, the Prophet's city. Beginning in the 1920s, he was also called the "Shaikhul Islam." This title was used by the Mughals to honor religious personalities; the Ottomans formalized it as a bureaucratic designation for a person in charge of the state's religious affairs. In the twentieth-century Indian context, it was an honorary title popularly accorded a scholar who was recognized as a leading authority in Islamic guidance. Maulana Madani's Deobandi colleague who supported the Pakistan movement, Maulana Shabbir Ahmad 'Usmani (1885–1949) was also called by *his* followers "Shaikhul Islam." The titles of some of the biographies of

Maulana Madani listed in the bibliography provide some of the other honorary designations that he was given as a mark of high regard. In contrast to these titles, Maulana Madani himself typically signed his letters as *nang-i aslaf*, "The Disgrace of the Predecessors." Finally, the Library of Congress catalog treats "Madani" as Husain Ahmad's "last name," and I have followed that practice here.

A note on transliteration: I have used the spelling of names of organizations following their own (most common) spelling; e.g. Jamiat Ulama-i-Hind, Jamaat-i-Islami, Tablighi Jamaat.

1

THE ARREST OF THE
"UNDESIRABLE INDIANS,"
1916

The Sharif of Mecca, newly installed thanks to a British-backed coup against the Ottoman sultan, knew what he had to do to please his patrons. On December 2, 1916, he dispatched his police officers to arrest Maulana Husain Ahmad Madani in the house where he was lodging in Mecca. Colonel C. Wilson, the British pilgrim officer and link to the Government of India's Criminal Intelligence Office, had summoned the Sharif to Jeddah where he directed him explicitly to apprehend not only Husain Ahmad but also several sojourners, "undesirable Indians," who had come to the Hijaz for pilgrimage. Husain Ahmad was a well-known and respected Islamic scholar, an Indian who had been resident in Arabia his whole adult life. Now implicated in an Islamic plot to involve the Ottomans against the British in India, he was destined for extended detention in an island prison camp on Malta on the grounds of sedition, when his crime, if crime it was, can better be called devotion.

To that point in his life, the critical impetus to Maulana Husain Ahmad's actions had been devotion, devotion to his family elders as well as to intellectual and spiritual mentors like the one he was linked to in 1916 (Madani 1953 (hereafter *Naqsh-i hayat*): I, 9–13). Foremost among these was his father, who in 1899 had decided to fulfill his heart's desire of living in the Prophet Muhammad's city of Medina. He had brought with him his large family, including Husain

Ahmad, his third son. Husain Ahmad was still a student at that point, in his final year of seminary training at the influential north Indian *madrasa*, the Darul 'Ulum at Deoband. Reluctant as he was, he could not resist his father's wishes.

In the ensuing seventeen years, Maulana Husain Ahmad had returned to India three times in order to meet with his spiritual guide and teachers, to get married, and to attend to other family business. He had even taught at the Deoband seminary for a year. But his real base was in the Holy Places, and, at the time of his arrest, as a man in his late thirties, he had overcome enormous odds to establish himself as a respected Islamic teacher, particularly learned in prophetic traditions or *hadith*. His circle of students, who were drawn from many countries, met in the Prophet's Mosque. In this he was a testimonial to the high quality of Indian scholarship in the cosmopolitan tradition of sacred Islamic learning. Husain Ahmad was also a responsible member of his family, which had faced great hardships in making the transition to another country.

The Holy Places of Mecca and Medina, located in the Ottoman province of the Hijaz, was home in those years to extensive networks of an Indian diaspora. It included Islamic scholars like Husain Ahmad, holy men with circles of disciples, as well as students who had come for the intellectual and spiritual blessing of residence in the Holy Places. Many individuals and schools in the Holy Cities were patronized by wealthy Indian aristocrats and traders. Maulana Husain Ahmad was among the recipients of Indian largesse, receiving in those years monthly stipends from two of the rulers whom the British called "princes," the pious woman grandee known as the Begum of Bhopal and the Nawab of Bahawalpur (L/PS/10/648 1917). The wealthy also supported facilities for the comfort of pilgrims. Shortly before their arrest, Husain Ahmad and his companions, for example, had found lodging in the port city of Jeddah in a hospice established by the ruler of Rampur state, another Indian prince. Another significant group within the Indian diaspora were traders, including a core group with ties to Delhi, and they, in fact, were often the conduit for transmitting charitable gifts from home.

Many were agents for India-based companies. Others were petty entrepreneurs, dealing in books, sweets, rosaries, and the like for the pilgrim market (PRO/TNA: FO686/149/ff. 202–208).

Traders, scholars, and patrons all had their bonds to India reinvigorated through their own travel and through visits from Indian pilgrims and others, especially after the introduction of steam travel in the late nineteenth century. In 1915, one of Maulana Husain Ahmad's revered teachers from Deoband, the luminous scholar and elder, Maulana Mahmudul Hasan (1851–1920), had led a group of pilgrims to Mecca. It was common for pilgrims to seek out an occasion to undertake the *hajj* with such a person in order to secure the additional blessing of his companionship while performing the sacred ritual. Husain Ahmad would later conclude that among Maulana Mahmudul Hasan's own group were loyalists to British colonial interests bent on currying favor, or prosecuting their own designs, by bringing harm to Maulana Mahmudul Hasan and the others. This was a reasonable surmise given the Kiplingesque cast of spies, "approvers," and "loyal" Indians evident in any perusal of colonial records in these years – and the disproportionate colonial fear of Muslim conspiracy.

In his book about the detention on Malta, *The Prisoner of Malta*, written in the guise of a travelogue about Mahmudul Hasan, Husain Ahmad provided details about the arrest (Madani n.d., hereafter *Asir-i malta*). The problem had to do with a declaration that reproduced an argument about Islamic authority initiated by the Arab Bureau in Cairo and other British officials claiming expertise in Islam. This argument was predicated on the assumption that there was a happy coincidence between British geo-political ambitions and "correct" Islamic interpretations. It denounced the Turks as infidels, *kafirs*. It also asserted that the "caliph," the holder of that ancient position linked to the earliest years of Islamic rule, and later adopted by the Ottoman sultan, could only be of Arab descent. It thus presumed to give complete legitimacy to the Sharif's revolt against the Ottoman overlord. It also assumed that "Islamic doctrine," not, for example, good governance, was all that any Muslim cared about. In fact, no Arab units of the Ottoman army ever came over to the Sharif; a few thousand tribesmen, paid off by British money and famous thanks to Colonel T. E. Lawrence, "Lawrence of Arabia," formed his troops (Fromkin 1990: 219).

The Indians in the Hijaz did not hesitate to speak out. Maulana Khalil Ahmad Ambahtawi (1852–1927), another of Maulana Husain Ahmad's revered Deobandi teachers, was described by the British agent as among those most outraged by the claims of the king:

> . . . this was the man who had told King Hussein to his face in Mecca in 1916 that his pretensions to the caliphate were presumptuous and would not be entertained in India, and many more unpalatable truths to the same effect. The king has never forgotten and is said to be extremely frightened of the moulvi, who is a very outspoken man, and who intends, so I am told, to give the king *un mauvais quart d'heure* at Mecca on the subject of the latter's intrigues and aspirations in the Islamic world [FO 868/26 1920].

With opinions like these circulating in India as well, colonial officials hoped somehow to turn the tide.

A declaration in support of the British argument was presented to Mahmudul Hasan and his companions on behalf of one Khan Bahadur Mubarak ʿAli, who had arrived from India to secure signatures from respected Islamic scholars of Mecca. Mubarak ʿAli gained the support of the Shaikhul Islam, the chief Meccan religious official, committed as he was to securing support for the Sharif. As his British title "Khan Bahadur" suggests, the Indian was, in Maulana Husain Ahmad's words, "a government man" (*Asir-i malta*: 58). Mubarak ʿAli particularly wanted signatures of well-known Indian scholars, and of these, apparently, none was more important than Maulana Mahmudul Hasan.

Not surprisingly, Mahmudul Hasan declined to add his signature to the declaration, advancing first what might be called the technical ground that the declaration was presented as the opinion of Meccan *ʿulama* teaching in the sanctuary. He did not hesitate, however, according to Maulana Husain Ahmad, to point out to the official that the justification of the Sharif's coup was clearly in conflict with *shari'a* law. Husain Ahmad prudently asked the official to report the technical demurral only. To no avail. He soon returned with a version that dropped the assertion of Ottoman unbelief. Maulana Mahmudul Hasan still refused to sign. At this point, the Khan Bahadur thought it best to leave for India with whatever signatures he had garnered. And Mahmudul Hasan concluded that he ought to get out of Mecca.

But before the group could secure transport, the head of the pilgrim guides – men licensed by the Hijaz government to take responsibility for foreign pilgrims – arrived at their lodging. He announced that their "government" (the English word was used), whose subjects they were, had summoned them. Maulana 'Uzair Gul, a disciple of Maulana Mahmudul Hasan from the Indian northwest frontier, burst out in indignation. He denied the legitimacy of any infidel government and claimed security in Mecca on the basis of its status as a sanctuary – as it had in fact been for Indian Muslims who had settled there during the brutal reprisals visited on Muslims after the uprising of 1857. The Arab official at this point retreated (*Asir-i malta*: 64).

What could they do? The group decided that Maulana Husain Ahmad with his fluent Arabic and good reputation should be the one to intercede with the Shaikhul Islam on the group's behalf. Sayyid Amin 'Asim, their own pilgrimage guide, agreed to go along. He would meet the Shaikhul Islam first and only then would Husain Ahmad speak. Amin 'Asim was apparently a man of great courtesy, as well as some Islamic learning himself. He of course had an interest in restoring good relations with the officials for the sake of his own reputation.

The Shaikhul Islam did not stand on ceremony. He greeted Husain Ahmad by saying that Mahmudul Hasan was the enemy of the Sharif's regime, heard even to call them "Kharijis," a term used for a group of dissidents active in the early centuries of Islam. Why else had he not signed? Husain Ahmad rehearsed the argument that Maulana Mahmudul Hasan and the rest *could not* sign because they were not Meccans. He then asked the Shaikh to give the group one more day until the Sharif himself returned to town so that they could meet him directly. The Shaikh responded by upping his accusations with the charge that Mahmudul Hasan was holding political meetings in the Sanctuary Mosque after the sunset prayer. Husain Ahmad denied this staunchly and insisted that Mahmudul Hasan only went to the mosque to teach and to pray. What about political discussion? Only about what was in the newspapers, Husain Ahmad insisted, and that too not about Arabia but affairs outside.

Maulana Husain Ahmad then found himself put on the spot since the Shaikh had gotten wind of a conversation in the shop of the Delhi trader, Hajji 'Abdul Jabbar, in which Husain Ahmad himself purportedly had denounced the extent of English control. Husain Ahmad insisted that the conversation was simply spurred by the arrival of someone with a book bound in the European style. He had indeed, he admitted, lamented that nowadays tastes ran only to what was European. When Husain Ahmad returned to his lodgings and recounted the conversation to the others, all agreed that they should use their day of grace to find a way to escape.

· When 'Abdul Jabbar, the Delhi trader, heard this plan, he thought it was a mistake. He urged the group instead to crave forgiveness in the most abject way from the Shaikhul Islam. Would Husain Ahmad be willing to kiss the official's hand and beg his pardon? Husain Ahmad did not hesitate a minute. If it would help Maulana Mahmudul Hasan, he said, he would kiss the Shaikh's feet. 'Abdul Jabbar went on ahead to the Shaikh's in-laws' house, where the Shaikh gathered with others every evening, and, in due course, Husain Ahmad followed and did exactly as 'Abdul-Jabbar suggested. He kissed the Shaikh's hand, begged forgiveness, and went off to sit quietly at the side of the room. According to Husain Ahmad, the Shaikh commented that whether it was right or wrong to fight the Turks, now that they had started, they had to continue. After coffee, the penitents returned home, optimistic that all had been settled.

But in the new context of British influence, the old formalities no longer worked. The Sharif insisted on an immediate arrest. When Husain Ahmad and the others got word of this, they decided that Mahmudul Hasan, accompanied by the youngest of their group,

Husain Ahmad's nephew Wahid Ahmad, should go off and hide. The others now hoped that if some of them spent a few days in jail, the matter could be resolved. When the police came they found Husain Ahmad alone and accordingly placed him under arrest. The commissioner greeted him with words that made clear who was behind his arrest: "You denounce the English; now you can have a taste of them" (*Asir-i malta*: 68). Arrests of the animated 'Uzair Gul and a second companion, the sober Hakim Nusrat Husain, followed. The bewildered Hakim thought that suspicion might have fallen on him, as well as on his nephew, who had actually left for India before the arrests took place, simply because of wholly innocent transfers of money they had made. The nephew would in fact be arrested and jailed upon his arrival in India.

The loyal Delhi traders went in delegation directly to the Sharif on behalf of the prisoners, insisting on their innocence and asking that at least they not be turned over to non-Muslims. Apparently the Sharif was frank enough to explain to them that at this point he simply could not offend the British over a matter like this. He announced immediately that if Mahmudul Hasan did not surrender himself that day, 'Uzair Gul and the Hakim would be shot dead; Mahmudul Hasan's pilgrimage guide would lose his license and be lashed. Maulana Mahmudul Hasan presented himself that evening, dressed in the *ihram* of the pilgrim as if he had simply gone outside Mecca in order to enter the city for ritual purposes. This stratagem was of no avail. He was taken directly to Jeddah under armed guard (*Asir-i malta*: 63–70).

MAULANA MAHMUDUL HASAN, DEOBAND, AND NEW POLITICAL STRATEGIES

Maulana Mahmudul Hasan was without doubt the most influential of the second generation of *'ulama* associated with the seminary at Deoband, a small town northeast of Delhi. The school had been founded in 1866 in the face of colonial repression after the great uprising of 1857. Mahmudul Hasan's father, a deputy inspector in the colonial educational service, had been one of those involved in the school's founding and subsequently served on its consultative council. The founders wanted to bring the structure, and even teaching techniques, of modern education to the transmission of the classic religious sciences even while eschewing the subject matter of the colonial schools. Deoband set the pattern for popularly funded schools that would transmit Islamic learning and practice independent of state control during the colonial period. Such innovations in all religious traditions in the colonial period fostered sectarian identities and disseminated religious teachings more widely than they had ever been before (Metcalf 2002).

Mahmudul Hasan was the school's legendary first student, completing his course of study in 1873. He subsequently served as teacher, becoming principal in 1890, and, upon the death of one of the school's founders in 1905, he took on the position of patron as well. He was primarily a scholar of *hadith*, of the traditions that narrate the acts and words of the Prophet Muhammad, and of Qur'an. Maulana Husain Ahmad called him "the seal of the *hadith* scholars," modeling the phrase on the epithet of Muhammad as "the seal of the prophets"; he was also "the chief of the Qur'an commentators" (*Asir-i malta*: 3). Knowledge was not a separate thing from holiness, but both were intimately linked in the confidence of his followers that he embodied prophetic teachings in a way that was unique for his time and perhaps even beyond. Although Maulana Mahmudul Hasan was not Husain Ahmad's Sufi *pir*, he was a powerful presence at every point in his life from school days until his own death. Husain Ahmad himself described him as someone with "a heart more expansive than the width of the seven seas; the seven climes could not locate themselves in even a corner . . ." (*Asir-i malta*: 7). Others remembered him as a small, intense man with piercing eyes (Minault 1982: 27).

What cause, then, was there for official suspicion of Maulana Mahmudul Hasan, the school, or its leadership in general? From the beginning the Deobandi *'ulama*, like virtually every other institutionalized group in British India in the late nineteenth century, had expressed their loyalty to the Crown in the aftermath of the brutally repressed rebellion of 1857. It was no small achievement to gain credibility for this stance given that Muslims were disproportionately blamed for the uprising and some of the 'ulama specifically targeted. The Deobandis as a group had not subsequently engaged in political activities at all, leaving to the western-educated the world of meetings, pamphlets, petitions, and addresses – the newly emerging framework of public life in the late nineteenth century. By the first decade of the new century, however, changes were afoot, notably in the large province of Bengal where nationalist protest and even terrorism were beginning to be felt after the 1905 decision, ostensibly on administrative grounds, to partition the province. The partition was seen as diminishing the political clout of Bengali political activists. It also created a Muslim-majority province in the east.

Westernized Muslim leaders were beginning to question British policy. They focused on a number of issues concerning the interests of Muslims, among them challenges to Urdu (written in a modified Arabic script) as the sole official vernacular language in the United Provinces; inadequate recognition of Muslims in governing councils; and the revocation of the Bengal partition in 1911. They were also troubled by British foreign policy in the Middle East. In regard to this last, some among the Muslim leadership saw with alarm the shift from support of the Ottomans (as a counter to Russians), which had been British policy at such points as the Russo-Turkish war of the 1870s, toward support of dissident Ottoman provinces, notably in the Tripolitan and Balkan wars of 1911–1913. There were now Urdu newspapers critical of government policy and new organizations like the "Servants of the Kaaba." This organization was intended principally to render service to pilgrims to the Holy Places, but it also concerned itself with threats to the Sultan's role as their protector.

Leadership in these activities for the most part was in the hands of the western-educated men associated with the English-medium college at Aligarh that had been founded in 1875. Husain Ahmad (testifying in apparent honesty after his arrest) pointed out that Deobandis had been puzzled when two of the chief organizers of the Kaaba

society came, unsuccessfully, to try to interest the 'ulama in participating. Deoband's rector, Maulana Hafiz Muhammad Ahmad, far
from political involvement, had even received the government title
of "Shamsul 'Ulama" (The Sun of the 'Ulama)."[The activists] are
what we call men of the new light (Nai Roshani)," Husain Ahmad
said, "and look down upon us as old-fashioned" (PRO/TNA:
FO686/149/ff. 208).

It is likely that Deobandis began to fall under suspicion because of
a single figure who had ties both to Deoband and to the political
activists, Maulana 'Ubaidullah Sindhi (1872–1944). In 1909–1910,
the leadership at Deoband, including Maulana Mahmudul Hasan,
hoping to consolidate the school's scholarly influence, decided to
bring a half dozen of their most able graduates back to the school,
among them Husain Ahmad and 'Ubaidullah Sindhi, an orphaned
Sikh who became a Muslim as a teenager and entered Deoband in
1888. Husain Ahmad's appointment at the school was soon made
permanent, to be resumed whenever he returned from Medina.
Both intellectually and financially, this was an excellent arrangement. He served as a teacher for a year, beginning late in 1909, his
only significant period in India between his initial departure and the
arrest described above.

In 1910 the school's leaders, as part of their new initiative at the
school, decided to hold a three-day convocation, a *dastarbandi* or
"tying of the turban" to recognize the accomplishment of graduates
by a visible symbol of accomplishment and authority. By this point,
there were over a thousand graduates of the school and the prospect
of accommodating as many of them as would come, as well as other
friends of the school, was a massive undertaking. Husain Ahmad's
own responsibility was to prepare students to deliver speeches in
Arabic. This specific event turned out to be somewhat manqué since
the audience demanded that the speakers switch to Urdu, but the
convocation as a whole was a great triumph, as widespread newspaper commentary apparently demonstrated. It initiated a successful
fund-raising campaign to build a new hostel, a mosque, and a separate library.

The occasion, according to Husain Ahmad, was filled with evidence of spiritual power and blessing that he took as evidence of the spiritual power (*batini tasarruf*) of Maulana Mahmudul Hasan. The event, however, drew official attention to the school. In the government's post-World War I report on alleged subversion it was singled out as a critical step in creating networks among politically suspect Muslims, with 'Ubaidullah Sindhi identified as the lynchpin of an alleged conspiracy and none other than Maulana Mahmudul Hasan as its animating presence (Minault 1982: 28–29).

Subsequent to the convocation, 'Ubaidullah Sindhi, with the support of Maulana Mahmudul Hasan, did indeed take the lead in seeking to institutionalize the bonds among graduates that the convocation had celebrated. To this end, he hoped to create an "old boys" organization, the Jami'atul Ansar, which met for the first time at the convocation itself. It held subsequent meetings in nearby towns with a view to creating a national organization for the Islamic schools. This was a project viewed sympathetically even by the most apolitical of the *'ulama* (Thanavi 2004). The organization, however, was to prove short-lived.

'Ubaidullah also apparently wanted to make changes within Deoband itself, training students in the arts of public speaking and writing. By 1913, however, members of the administration of the school, represented in particular by Hafiz Muhammad Ahmad, were nervous about 'Ubaidullah's potentially jeopardizing the school's long-term priority of being scrupulously apolitical. Many of the Deobandi leadership, moreover, grew uneasy with 'Ubaidullah's seeming modernist deviation from the traditionalist Hanafi orientation central to the school's identity. This deviation was the spur to asking him to leave.

Moving to Delhi, 'Ubaidullah turned his attention to founding yet another organization, in this case a Qur'anic school, the Nizaratul Ma'ariful Quraniyya, intended to provide religious education for those educated in English-medium schools like Aligarh. This was welcomed by leading figures among the more westernized Muslims, including Dr. M. A. Ansari (1880–1936), a western-trained physician whose family had old ties to the Deobandis, and Hakim Ajmal Khan (1863–1927), a physician in the Greco-Arabic medical system who was active in systematizing and "modernizing" traditional medical knowledge and instruction. Both were public figures involved in a medical mission to the Balkans, but both also sustained good ties to British officials (*Naqsh-i hayat*: II, 144).

Maulana Mahmudul Hasan quietly kept his relationship with 'Ubaidullah intact and favored his educational initiatives. The British report issued after the War alleged that Deoband, along with 'Ubaidullah's organizations, was a center for anti-British political organizing in this pre-war period (Bamford [1925]: 122–125). This seems not to have been the case but rather reflected British anxiety about Muslim subversion. Even much later, when Deobandis and others wanted to emphasize their anti-colonial activities, no one claimed any anti-British dimension to these pre-war activities.

'Ubaidullah Sindhi's political thinking was not formed, he himself would later write, until he had spent several years in Delhi working with westernized leaders concerned about British policies both outside and inside India. In addition to Dr. Ansari and Hakim Ajmal Khan, he interacted with rising political figures like the journalist and theologian Abul Kalam Azad (1888–1958), who had been part of anti-British activist circles in Bengal early in the century, and a second journalist, Muhammad 'Ali (1878–1931), a graduate of Aligarh (Minault 1982: 30–31).

THE WAR AND THE "SILK LETTER CONSPIRACY"

With Britain's declaration of war against Turkey, and the Ottoman Sultan's subsequent proclamation of *jihad* on November 14, 1914, in response, the pace of political life in Delhi intensified. Within India, the cost of war was enormous, not least in the sacrifice of Indian troops deployed in the Middle East. Almost immediately upon the declaration of war, for example, British Indian troops successfully occupied Basra (in contemporary Iraq). A subsequent march toward Baghdad, however, proved a disastrous undertaking in terms of logistics and deficiencies in every form of support. More than half the forces of about 9000 men were lost. A last stand was made at Kut, with reinforcements deployed as wastefully as they had been in the initial assault; there were over 30,000 casualties. The human cost of the Great War, generally, was enormous. In January 1915, the Ottoman general, Anwar (or Enver) Pasha (1881–1922), led his troops east, hoping to crush Russia and, apparently, march via Afghanistan to conquer India; of his troops, perhaps 86 percent were lost. The next spring saw the unprecedented, disastrous campaign in the Dardanelles, masterminded by the same H. H. Kitchener (1850–1916) who had fought the Mahdi of the Sudan. Each side suffered an incredible estimated 250,000 casualties (Fromkin 1990: 201–203, 120–121, 166). According to Husain Ahmad, Maulana Mahmudul Hasan came to believe that the Christian world was intent on extinguishing Islam, just as had happened to Judaism throughout the world and Islam in Spain and Portugal. This was a time of great destruction, he explained, in the Balkans, Iraq, Syria, Armenia – and the Hijaz (*Asir-i malta*: 11–13).

In the Hijaz, the declaration of war had brought huge public meetings to urge participation on the Turkish side, but the Sharif increasingly saw his interests served by siding with the British. By the summer of 1916, as noted above, he had gone into open revolt. Meanwhile, Maulana Mahmudul Hasan, still in India, had, in the preceding year, interacted with 'Ubaidullah Sindhi over a plan for the latter to proceed to India's northwest frontier to play a role in whatever anti-British opposition would emerge. It was not implausible to think that a challenge to British rule could come from the northwest, given its endemic resistance to centralized governments, culminating in the post-World War I Third Afghan War. For 'Ubaidullah, moreover, there were Deobandi students from the area with whom he could hope to establish connections.

The Government of India feared Maulana Mahmudul Hasan's influence, given the large number of his disciples and especially the substantial numbers of former students located in the frontier. He had also refused to sign an earlier declaration (*fatwa*) in favor of the overthrow of the Ottoman sultan circulated within India shortly before his departure for the Hijaz. By the summer of 1915, Dr. Ansari, who had contacts in the government, became concerned that Maulana Mahmudul Hasan's arrest was imminent. He urged him to leave India and he himself made arrangements for the trip (Muhammad Miyan 2005: 38).

The government report alluded to above, the Sedition (Rowlatt) Committee Report, no doubt exaggerated the importance of the activities on the frontier. Moreover, it implied a "Mahomedan" dimension to the events there which is belied by the international and secular non-Muslim participation that the report itself documented. The chimera of Muslim "fanatics" on the frontier was a continuing thread in colonial ideology from the late nineteenth century on, even if belied by lack of evidence.

Political activism during the Great War had two other sources. Frontier tribes were typically motivated to oppose centralized state control (including control by Muslim-dominated states). As for 'Ubaidullah, the spur to his activism came not from his religious mentors but from the early nationalists, journalists, and organizers in Delhi, linked by their knowledge of English to dissident elites in other parts of India and to international news from the Middle East and Europe. A stream of militant anti-British activism, and even terrorism, began to take shape in India and the Indian diaspora from the turn of the century. This was spearheaded not by Muslims but by Indians of Hindu, Sikh, and even Parsi background

As described in the Rowlatt Committee Report (in Bamford [1925]: 122–125), 'Ubaidullah, with three companions, had gone to the frontier in August 1915 in order to spread "a pan-Islamic and anti-British movement" through "maulvis" trained at Deoband. After 'Ubaidullah arrived at the frontier, he visited "the Hindustani fanatics" before carrying on to Kabul where he met members of a Turco-German mission. Meanwhile, one of Maulana Mahmudul Hasan's traveling companions had returned from the Hijaz in 1916, the

Report claimed, with a declaration of *jihad* from Ghalib Pasha, the Turkish military governor of the Hijaz, intended for distribution both in India and among the frontier tribes to encourage their support.

'Ubaidullah and his fellow conspirators, the Report continued, had devised a scheme for the provisional government of India after the overthrow of British power, led by one Mahendra Pratap. The Report described him as "a Hindu of good family and eccentric character" and said that in Geneva he had met founders of the Ghadar Party (another anti-British scheme strong on the west coast of the United States). The "Provisional Government" had invited both the Governor of Russian Turkestan and the Czar of Russia to end their alliance with Great Britain and assist in the overthrow of British rule in India. 'Ubaidullah wrote to Maulana Mahmudul Hasan outlining his plan, and it was this letter, neatly and clearly written on yellow silk, that fell into British hands. The letter gave a detailed tabular statement of the projected "Army of God" and a list of people who might serve in the projected government. Once the letter was discovered, in August 1916, the British were determined to arrest Maulana Mahmudul Hasan and the other "conspirators" with him.

Maulana Mahmudul Hasan's role seems to have been one of moral support to anti-British activity on the frontier and possibly some ineffective attempts to garner Ottoman efforts against British rule in India. There seems to have been no evidence about any of his four companions, only guilt by association, even though Husain Ahmad, to be sure, had expressed his commitment to Ottoman rule in the Hijaz. For Husain Ahmad, it was only Maulana Mahmudul Hasan's arrival that gave direction to his growing understanding of European misgovernment and exploitation and his emerging drive to challenge British rule (*Naqsh-i hayat*: II, 215–216). Even less involved was Hakim Nusrat Husain, who was arrested precisely because of a hope that he would be a "mole" to reveal the plotting of the others. In the event, Nusrat Husain, a young man in his twenties, would sicken in the harsh conditions of Malta and die. It was devotion to Maulana Mahmudul Hasan, rather than any active involvement in whatever scheme there may or may not have been, that led to the arrests. Such deep affective ties of loyal devotion, often expressed through Sufi initiation, are critical to understanding not only individual spiritual life but the unfolding of socio-political life in India as well.

With the arrest, Husain Ahmad began to develop a new political consciousness in relation to colonial rule (*Naqsh-i hayat*: I, 129–131). He saw the coup of the Sharif, though glossed by the British as the triumph of Arab nationalism, as nothing more than a strategy to allow the British scope for their own policies. That the rhetoric of freeing Middle Eastern peoples from a tyrannous regime masked other goals would become clearer with revelations like the post-war exposure of the secret Sykes–Picot Agreement of 1916, which threw the war's slogan of "self-determination" to the wind and carved up the region into British and French spheres of control. For Maulana Husain Ahmad, his political education and his ties to Maulana Mahmudul Hasan went hand in hand. The years of detention that followed his arrest shaped the two interdependent themes at the core of his activities in the decades that would follow: immersion in Islamic learning and spirituality, and anti-colonial activism.

2

"THE PRISONER OF MALTA," 1916–1920

Maulana Mahmud Hassan, son of Zulfikar Ali, aged 70:

> ... He should be treated as a political detenu who has been against us from religious conviction & not as a common self-seeking conspirator ... It is desired that his presence ... should not become known to the public ... to ensure this, such precautions as are possible should be taken.

Maulvi Hussain Ahmad, son of Habibullah, aged 38:

> ... there is no doubt that any young Moslem coming in contact with him would be in danger of being converted to his views & of becoming disloyal ... Besides being dangerous in this way he is an energetic man quite capable of taking an active part in politics under a religious disguise ...

Auzer Gul, son of Shahid Gul, age 26:

> This man accompanied Maulana Mahmud Hassan on the S.S. Akbar. He is an irreconcileable hater ... & requires very strict supervision & control. There is no reason to show him consideration as in the case of the old Maulana. ...

Wahid Ahmad, son of Siddik Ahmad, age 20:

> This youth is the nephew of Hussain Ahmad. He came with the Maulana on the S.S. Akbar as a disciple & servant. He is a child in

mind, ready to carry out blindly whatever his religious master orders. He is the type of youth used by anarchists to commit political murder. Left alone he is harmless.

Hakim Nasrat Hussain, son of Sayyid Zain-ul-Abdin, age 28:

> . . . This young man was possibly not concerned in the conspiracy but he was living in the same building with the Maulana's party . . . & has been treated as belonging to it. He has had some education in the Moslem school of medicine & surgery . . . besides religious instruction in Deoband. His religious views are those of the Maulana, of whom he is a great admirer. In politics he has reason to be pro-British. It is possible that he may be induced by tactful treatment to divulge what he knows, if indeed he knows anything, about the conspiracy from the inside. All his correspondence should be sent to the Arab Bureau, Cairo, pending further instructions . . .
>
> [Arab Bureau Notes on Husain Ahmad and
> Fellow Internees at Malta, 1917]

The interrogation that would produce this record lay ahead. Now, still imprisoned in a cell alone in Mecca, Maulana Husain Ahmad waited to learn what had befallen his beloved teacher. After two weeks, he heard the news: Maulana Mahmudul Hasan had also been arrested. Husain Ahmad implored one of those who came to tell him, a cousin of the pilgrim guide, to intercede for him to accompany Maulana Mahmudul Hasan if they took him anywhere other than India. It was soon clear that the authorities clearly intended nothing else. They told him to collect his belongings, took him to Jeddah by mule under armed escort, and placed him in a cell with Maulana Mahmudul Hasan.

Maulana Mahmudul Hasan's first order of business was not conspiracy but his dream of the previous night:

> Before me was the bier of the Prophet. We all had been brought there. I understood that it was I who was to undertake all the responsibilities of shrouding, burying, and so forth. In my heart of hearts, I could not understand how I could do all this. Then I saw that the bier was placed to one side and Hazrat Hajji Imdadullah [1817–1899, the eminent

Indian *shaikh,* his own Sufi guide] . . .was sitting on his knees in
meditation in front of him, and I was going about on all sides making
the arrangements . . . [*Asir-i malta*: 72]

This dream, like any dream of the Prophet or other holy figure, was
understood to have absolute validity. It clearly indicated the favor of
the Prophet by his granting such an opportunity of service. It conveyed the blessing of Hajji Imdadullah, and it gave assurance to
Maulana Mahmudul Hasan and his companions that they could face
the challenges ahead. Other sustaining dreams in the course of the
detention would follow.

That night, one Baha'uddin, the British-appointed Protector of
Pilgrims, came to inform them that a steamer would leave for Cairo
the next day. Claiming to speak in good faith to him as an Indian and
fellow Muslim, the prisoners told him that it would be a mistake to
send them back to India, which is what they assumed was happening,
since they would freely tell everyone what was going on in the Hijaz.
The next day, Baha'uddin returned with the news that according to
Colonel Wilson the Sharif required that they be sent to Egypt. At this,
the two somewhat desperately insisted that it would be better for
them to be sent to India, but this was now out of the question.
Baha'uddin lodged them on the top floor of his own accommodation,
with soldiers of the Sharif stationed on the ground below. In the end,
they spent a month there while officials debated their ultimate fate.

On January 12, 1917, the five Indians were dispatched to Egypt by
steamer. Four days later, they landed at Suez, were settled in tents,
and guarded by Indian soldiers (whose numbers in the Middle East
had increased because of the war). The next day, under an armed
escort of Europeans, they were taken by train to Cairo and directly to
a long-disused prison, recently reclaimed for use for some 200 political prisoners. They were searched and registered, and their knives
and other items were taken from them along with the cash that they
had brought from Mecca. They were lodged in tents within the
prison walls, grateful for the warm clothes that they had brought
with them from Mecca against the winter chill.

THE TRIBUNAL

In the morning the prisoners were taken by tram to the war offices in the city and separately faced three British officials, of whom two spoke excellent Urdu. A. B. fforde (sic), long posted as an Indian Civil Service officer to the United Provinces and deputed to Egypt earlier that year, led the interrogation. The officers had before them a thick printed file of intelligence, dealing in particular with Maulana Mahmudul Hasan. Both Maulana Mahmudul Hasan and Maulana Husain Ahmad completely denied any subversive activity. Husain Ahmad's later account of the events, when he had no fear of British reprisals, in fact gave a more political gloss to their earlier encounters with the Ottoman officials in the Hijaz than he did on this occasion.

Whatever the content, the dialogue is significant for Maulana Mahmudul Hasan's cavalier lack of deference to his rulers. When told that 'Ubaidullah said he was part of his conspiracy against British rule as a military "commander," Maulana Mahmudul Hasan replied: "[That's] his say-so. Me, a military commander? Look at my age and the shape I'm in! Have I ever had anything to do with warfare?" To the suggestion that he had secured a letter from the military governor of the Hijaz, Ghalib Pasha, Maulana Mahmudul Hasan continued his dismissive tone: "You tell me: how is an ordinary person like me going to meet the governor of the Hijaz? I don't know him, I don't know Turkish, and I've had no previous contact with Turkish officials . . ." He acknowledged meeting Anwar Pasha and Jamal Pasha (the Turkish foreign minister and governor of the Hijaz, respectively) in an assembly of 'ulama in Medina where, in fact, Maulana Husain Ahmad spoke, but he completely dismissed the suggestion of interacting with the Turks to foment an attack on India on the part of Turkey, Iran, and Afghanistan: "I am astonished that you, who have been ruling a country for so long, can think that the voice of an unknown person like me could reach to kings, let alone remove long years of enmity between these countries. And if I did, would they have soldiers to spare to go off to India to fight a war . . .?" (PRO/TNA: FO686/149/ff. 202–208). The questioning continued for two more days, with each of the other four Indians appearing separately.

According to the British transcript, Maulana Husain Ahmad said, "I never intrigued against the Sherif on the side of the Turks, nor was I ever accused of doing so. I have never meddled with politics." He insisted that he had "no political views regarding British rule in India," and he invoked his deep bond to Maulana Mahmudul Hasan as explanation for why he "took care of Maulana Mahmud Hassam [sic] all the time he was in the Hijaz" (PRO/TNA: FO686/149/ff. 202–208).

As for Anwar Pasha and Jamal Pasha, Maulana Husain Ahmad explained that when they had come to Medina, the Hanafi Mufti had asked him, among others, to preach, and he chose for him the subject of the religious dimension of *jihad*. His sermon, he said, acknowledging his typical loquaciousness, was cut off before he had finished. He, like the other speakers, was paid five guineas. He went on to explain that he in fact did prefer Turkish rule to that of the Sharif on the ground that the Turks were more just and more generous, whereas the Sharif "beats and imprisons without inquiry," even, he said, killing children and outraging women. In relation to 'Ubaidullah, Maulana Husain Ahmad said, plausibly:

> I swear most solemnly that I had no suspicion that there were any secret political aims in the [Jamiat al Ansar]. Obedullah had great dreams of making Deoband the centre of Moslem thought and influence. I was against his grandiose scheme pointing out that there were no funds to carry them out. The masters thought that Obedullah was striving to obtain complete ascendency [sic] over the school, but none suspected anything more . . . [PRO/TNA: FO686/149/f. 204].

Maulana Husain Ahmad never retracted this affirmation of his own lack of political involvement before the outbreak of the war and the subsequent arrival of Maulana Mahmudul Hasan in the Hijaz. Similarly, it appears plausible that before his shift to the northwest frontier in 1915, 'Ubaidullah's interests were primarily directed toward enhancing the role of the *'ulama* within the cultural life of India, even as his interactions with journalists like Abul Kalam Azad and Muhammad 'Ali drew him into politically activist circles. At the tribunal, Maulana Husain Ahmad attributed rumors about himself to the attempt of enemies in the Hijaz (the "Barelwis," discussed in Chapter 3) to spread rumors about them.

Hakim Nusrat Husain in his interrogation earnestly described himself to the investigators as "a government zamindar" who spent his time "in court cases, and so forth" – a telling comment to describe the pervasive adversarial legal culture produced by land policies in British India. He proclaimed himself someone ready to speak of government injustice in the spirit of a "well-wisher" of their rule (*Asir-i malta*: 93–94). The Hakim, alone of the five, spoke English, a useful skill in the years ahead. 'Uzair Gul was particularly pressed on specific figures active in the unrest in his home area on the northwest frontier, Yaghistan.

During the investigation, although Mahmudul Hasan and the Hakim were in a cell together, the others were each lodged in separate dark cells, initially allowed one hour alone morning and evening in the veranda each day, with no idea where the others were. All feared the worst. According to Husain Ahmad, these were in fact the worst days of the entire internment. Maulana Mahmudul Hasan, he wrote, particularly suffered from remorse that the others were at risk of execution because of him. Throughout, he continued, none ever wished to be anywhere except in the company of Maulana Mahmudul Hasan and, in the presumed face of execution, none was distraught, even out of concern for those left behind. 'Uzair Gul, the high-spirited Pathan, even practiced wearing a noose to insure that he would be ready for execution. Their calm, Maulana Husain Ahmad explained, was owed to the spiritual blessing of Maulana Mahmudul Hasan (*Asir-i malta*: 84–94).

TRAVEL

In the end, the decision was made to intern the five detainees together on the Mediterranean island of Malta, apart from other political prisoners more commonly transported from India to the Andaman Islands. The group was taken into Cairo for the double indignity of photographing and fingerprinting, surveillance techniques developed in the colonies, as well as for filling out forms in order to secure "passports." Photographs had become routine for transported Indian prisoners as early as 1875, preferably against a grid and in profile; fingerprinting, espoused as a way to circumvent a presumed Indian penchant for impersonation, was introduced somewhat later (Singha 1998: 173, 192). The case against the Indians was deemed not to merit execution, but Malta, they were later told by Turks they met, was intended as a destination for the most dangerous prisoners, the ones most opposed to the British and their allies (*Asir-i malta*: 112). Certainly in this case it was intended to prevent the Indians from exercising any influence within India. In mid-February 1917 the prisoners were taken by car to the Cairo train station, thence to Alexandria, and finally to the ship that would take them to Malta. There were European guards placed to watch them at every stage.

The week on ship provided an intimate opportunity to form an opinion of the Turks. The Indians seem to have found the Turks, high and low, to be kindhearted and gracious. To the astonishment of the Indians, the Turkish soldiers danced and sang in the evenings. They explained to Maulana Mahmudul Hasan and others that they meant no disrespect by this but that they danced to defy the British. Their shared political stance and mutual respect made for strong bonds between the Indian and Turkish prisoners during the internment, however different their national backgrounds might be and despite the seeming cultural contrast between the traditionalist scholars and the modernizing Turks.

The days at sea were punctuated by frequent lifeboat drills since all ships during this war were in constant danger. The group's conviction of the charismatic power of the sainted dead was evident. Maulana Mahmudul Hasan carried with him fragments of hair, fingernails, and pieces of cloth from his own *shaikh*, "the Lodestar of the World," Hajji Imdadullah; "the Sun of Islam," Maulana

Muhammad Qasim Nanautawi, his own revered teacher; and "the Sun of the *'Ulama* and the Learned," Maulana Rashid Ahmad Gangohi, his predecessor as Deoband's patron and Maulana Husain Ahmad's own revered Sufi *shaikh*. He distributed these relics (*tabarrukat*) to his four companions, no doubt a consolation to them but also a strategy so that, should only some of the five survive, not all the relics would be lost. Maulana Husain Ahmad received a piece of cloth worn by Rashid Ahmad (his *kamri*), given to Maulana Mahmudul Hasan at his time of death. It was a treasure that Maulana Husain Ahmad, even after the safe arrival on the island of Malta, never returned (*Asir-i malta*: 112–114).

The cataclysmic events of the weeks at the turn of the year, 1916 to 1917, exemplify the two streams of activities characteristic of Maulana Husain Ahmad's years on Malta and the four decades of his life that would follow. Through all, there would be both the experience of public political life as well as a distinctive world of intense individual and group spiritual commitments. In these weeks he demonstrated the leadership that he seemed naturally to assume, whether as intercessor with the Sharif's officials or as Maulana Mahmudul Hasan's primary support from among his many disciples.

MALTA

On February 21, 1917, the prisoners reached Malta. The officers and Maulana Mahmudul Hasan were transported to the camp, along with the luggage, by car. The four other Indians and the ordinary soldiers were held on ship until evening, at which point they proceeded to the camp by foot. Malta had had over two hundred years of Arab rule from 870 to 1090, and there remained hints of that past in Norman-Sicilian architecture and in the names of the old capital, "Mdina," and its suburb, "Rabat." In 1530 the Emperor Charles V awarded the island to the Knights Hospitalers (henceforth known as the Knights of Malta) whose history, from their founding in Jerusalem in the eleventh century, had been primarily focused on crusades. In 1798,

Napoleon took the island, holding it until British conquest in 1814. Now on Malta the quiescent crusade tradition was revived in opposition to "the Saracen" in the form of the Ottoman Turks.

Husain Ahmad would spend most of his more than three years in the shadow of the sixteenth-century fortification built by the crusaders, but he seems to have never reflected on the lost glories of Arab civilization or the romance of Saladin against Europe. There were many varied streams of Islamic political and cultural thought in British India. Historical romanticism in colonial India was more the purview of the more westernized, the writers of new-style historical novels, captivated by the example of Sir Walter Scott, like 'Abdul Halim Sharar (1860–1926), or of evocative poetry about Andalusia, like Muhammad Iqbal, so influenced by German romanticism. Maulana Husain Ahmad's emerging political consciousness would be focused on the present, on the material, and on the nitty-gritty of power, not on a romanticized historical past.

Maulana Husain Ahmad's memoir of the detention, written in prison after his arrest in India in 1921, provides rich detail on the experience of detainees on the island, even sketches of the camp layout and floor plans of buildings. The 3000 or so prisoners were strictly guarded, and the camp surrounded by barbed wire. About half of the prisoners were German; others included Austrians, Bulgarians, Turks, Egyptians, and Syrians. After the first uncomfortable month, lodged only in tents during very cold weather, the Indians were shifted to a room large enough to divide by a curtain. The outer space held a large table used for books and often cigarettes, chairs, and a wooden bed. In the inner room there was a bed under a glassed-in window where Maulana Mahmudul Hasan liked to sit to meditate or work; in the warm weather he used a bed placed outside. There was a large iron fireplace for heat.

To the east were two rooms housing perhaps two dozen Syrians from the coastal city of Sayda (the ancient city of Sidon, now in Lebanon). In the room on the west, they organized a mosque, spreading out government-supplied blankets on the floor, used by both them and the Syrians. The room had piped water that served

both for clothes washing and for ablutions. In front of the building
was a courtyard and beyond that space for gardens where the Syrians
and 'Uzair Gul grew vegetables. There were also fruit trees. Finally,
there was a ring of sheds, behind which stretched three rows of
barbed wire and the fortress wall. The Syrians put a tent pole in the
center of the courtyard and raised the Ottoman flag on Fridays, holidays, and occasions of Ottoman victories (*Asir-i malta*: 149–153).

The camp was conducted on the basis of international norms for
prisoners of war, and, in fact, everyone appears to have been treated
with decency.

The Indians found two fellow countrymen already in the camp, a
Punjabi Muslim doctor, who claimed to have been turned over to the
British by people in Cairo who had some grievance against him, and
a Bengali Brahman, "Mister Sidar," accused of terrorism, apparently
on no evidence at all. They received permission to lodge together, an
arrangement that lasted through most of that year (*Asir-i malta*: 136).
Camp authorities also accommodated a Turk condemned to die for
killing a fellow Turkish prisoner. When he heard that a holy person-
age had arrived at the camp, he asked to meet Maulana Mahmudul
Hasan, a wish that was granted and led to regular visits. At the time of
the execution, the guards provided tea and transport for the mourn-
ers, and the body was suitably laid to rest in the Islamic cemetery
built earlier by the Ottoman sultan. Prisoners were permitted to
visit among the half-dozen or so camps on a limited basis, and to go
out under supervision for recreational walks and even swims.
Officers or the elderly could hire horse carts for the outings (*Asir-i
malta*: 126–138).

One censored letter could be sent out twice weekly on regulation
lined paper as well as up to three postcards (to be purchased by the
prisoners). Maulana Husain Ahmad feared that he would bring suspicion on anyone, other than family members, to whom he chose to
write, and there were many delays in sending and receiving mail. In
his letters to Maulana Hafiz Zahid Husain Amrohawi, a disciple of
Hajji Imdadullah, who had known Husain Ahmad and his brothers
from their school days, he would sometimes joke about not hearing

from him. He called him his "esteemed and revered forgetful Hafiz Sahib" and, on another occasion, asked if he had sniffed some "snuff of silence" (Madani 1951: II, 71, 76, 78). But such lightness did not belie the worries of prisoners about those at home.

Officers and some high-ranking civilians were accorded relatively comfortable surroundings, sufficient salaries (to be reimbursed in due course by their own countries), and the services of ordinary soldiers. The officers, and a venerable figure like Maulana Mahmudul Hasan, were not required to line up with the others each morning but rather were counted in their dwellings. Prisoners were expected to sweep and clean their own quarters, but even the Indians were able to hire a Syrian sailor to look after their chores of clothes washing, cleaning, and fetching the daily ration of food (which they supplemented with their own purchases). They cooked their own food, and they seem to have eaten adequately although frugally (*Asir-i malta*: 163–166). At one point, one of the Turkish officers insisted on providing them with resources (which they took as loans), as did others. Some prisoners depended on parcels sent by the Red Cross and the Red Crescent, the latter received by the Turkish officers, who, according to Maulana Husain Ahmad, made no distinction of country or religion in distributing them (*Asir-i malta*: 129).

Considerable energy went into the practicalities of everyday life. Some found ways to build additional structures. Some made a business of serving other prisoners' needs: there were provisions stores, a coffee shop, and even a business making cigars. Others worked as washermen, cooks, or general servants. About ten months into their internment, Maulana Mahmudul Hasan was summoned to the commander's office to be told that under orders from the Government of India he was henceforth to be treated as if he were an army captain. He was invited to make requests for any needs he might have, and offered the opportunity, which he declined, to move to a camp that was more comfortable.

In early 1918, the Indian prisoners were again interrogated, this time by a Mr. Burn, who, they later learned, had been sent by James Meston, governor of the United Provinces, in response to a request from a delegation of *'ulama* petitioning for their release. This was in fact Sir Richard Burn (1871–1947), a member of the Indian Civil Service, whose obituary noted his considerable experience in agrarian matters, including famine relief, and his pursuit of a scholarly interest in the Mughal Empire in retirement (*The Times*, July 29, 1947: 6). Husain Ahmad reported that Burn spoke Urdu and knew Persian. He brought with him letters from several of their Deobandi colleagues. He was unfailingly courteous during his encounters, shaking hands, offering chairs, and inquiring about their health. Manners aside, he had been instructed to determine whether the prisoners were "repentant" – without specifying for what (FO 371/3046; FO 371/3396/f.57).

Burn questioned the five detainees in the prison offices and in their lodging as well, meeting them first as a group and then individually. He particularly asked Maulana Mahmudul Hasan his judgment about whether India was "*dar al islam*" or "*dar al harb*," reiterating the colonial anxiety, dating back to W. W. Hunter's alarmist inquiries of the 1870s, which were published in a much circulated pamphlet on this same issue (Hunter 1871). Maulana Mahmudul Hasan's answers as recorded by Husain Ahmad reflect the nuanced subtlety of a learned, traditionalist scholar exploring the possibilities of different interpretations. Burn understood him to deny that India was *dar al-harb*, to oppose *jihad*, and to regard *hijrat* in the current circumstances as not incumbent. Burn's very focus on "religion," however, reveals an enduring western blinder that looks to sacred texts, not geo-politics, to explain political behavior of Muslims.

According to Maulana Husain Ahmad, 'Uzair Gul just brushed off such questions: "Do you think I'm a Muslim? Doesn't a Muslim believe in the Qur'an? Then why are you asking me about *jihad*?" (*Asir-i malta*: 186). Burn had been forewarned (by the director of Central Intelligence in India) that 'Uzair Gul was "a really dangerous fanatic" but he found him not even looking like an "ordinary Pathan" with his fair skin, brownish beard, and ready smile. 'Uzair Gul denied any knowledge of any political activity in his native frontier. Throughout, Burn wrote, "the strongest note was one of personal devotion to the Maulana," summed up by the young Wahid Ahmad's comment that he wanted to be wherever the Maulana was, "the holiest man in the world" (OIOC L/P&S/10/648. P 5006/17).

Maulana Husain Ahmad explained the contacts that he, Maulana Mahmudul Hasan, and Maulana Khalil Ahmad had had with Turkish officials in the preceding year as an attempt to convince them that they were not anti-Turkish, a rumor planted by their enemies and plausible since they were assumed to be British subjects. In fact, Husain Ahmad pointed out, he was *not* British but a Turkish subject as a long-time resident of Medina and hence "at war with the British," no doubt a satisfying claim given his emerging anti-colonialism and perhaps a way to attempt to gain leverage as a prisoner of war, not a political prisoner (OIOC L/P&S/10/648. P 5006/17).

Ever practical, he also managed to use the questioning to review the concrete problems faced by the prisoners in light of what he called the unjustness of their imprisonment in the first place. He unfavorably compared the conditions in Malta to the conditions his brother reported in the Turkish prison in Adrianople, where he was imprisoned as a British subject. According to letters he had received, his brother was paid a more generous stipend, families were accommodated, and greater freedom of movement permitted. Burn was skeptical but Maulana Husain Ahmad bolstered his argument by reference to Britain's harsh treatment of Iraqi and other prisoners generally as he had heard from other prisoners. Burn did make notes and said he would present these issues to Parliament. Retelling this episode, once again in prison some three years later, Husain Ahmad made clear his evolving interpretation of the balance of world power:

> . . . the poor Turks were Asian, not Europeans; Muslim, not Christian; weak, not strong. So their good deeds became bad; their kindness, oppression . . . what I heard with my own ears made my hairs stand on end . . . When I think of it, I am astonished at God's forbearance and fail to understand why the earth does not open and the sky break . . . how long . . . will the blood of God's creation be the victim of their sharp and harsh fangs? O Allah, be the Helper and Friend of your weak servants. Oh Provider, protect your true religion. Oh Lord, correct

us. Erase from the earth our enemies as you did Pharaoh, Haman, Qarun, Namrud, Shaddad [*Asir-i malta*: 184–185].

Europe's habit, he wrote, in a judgment that many others would also make in the decades that followed, is to enforce the law on the weak but to dress the law in new meanings according to their whim when they themselves act (*Asir-i malta*: 183).

Burn spoke at length with Hakim Nusrat Husain on two occasions, seemingly in a quite different vein. Burn mostly talked to him about the district, agricultural issues, and his specific problems of managing his land and obligations from afar. It was to Hakim Nusrat Husain that he explained who he was and that he had stopped on his way to England on leave. He revealed that Baha'uddin, the official they had encountered in Jeddah, had recommended Hakim Nusrat Husain's release and he said that he would do the same. Hakim Nusrat Husain replied he would not leave Malta until all his companions were also released. When Hakim Nusrat Husain reported this to the others, they urged him to accept the offer, given his poor health and the opportunity he would have to work for their release in India (*Asir-i malta*: 191–193).

Burn failed to link Hakim Nusrat Husain's unwillingness to leave to the deep bonds among the prisoners. Rather he took this as evidence of guilt: that Hakim Nusrat Husain "though not associated at the earlier stages . . . ha[d] now become privy" to the conspiracy. He recommended against his release, as well as against the release of the others, explicitly arguing that release would allow Maulana Mahmudul Hasan in particular to "return with the added glory of a martyr and his reputation greatly increased." He urged great care in examining all parcels, the seams of clothing, and so forth that they might receive from India (OIOC L/P&S/10/648. P 5006/17). For all his civil behavior with the prisoners, Burn's report in fact made their release less likely, even if some minor improvement in their arrangements were secured.

Later that same year Hakim Nusrat Husain entered the camp hospital and died shortly thereafter, perhaps a victim of the influenza pandemic of 1918. The doctors, fearing infection, curtailed contacts but ultimately allowed his colleagues to visit and even, at Maulana Mahmudul Hasan's urgent insistence, carry out their obligations of burial preparations. The Turkish Colonel, Ashraf Beg, who was often helpful to the Indians, engraved a tombstone for the Hakim, to be placed with other memorials to those who had died on the island. Husain Ahmad would later sadly write that Hakim Nusrat Husain was a steadfast and faithful person (*Asir-i malta*: 177).

As Maulana Husain Ahmad's testimony makes clear, he increasingly came to condemn the larger institutions in which European actions were embedded, summed up for him in the injustice of this detention. He acutely observed the toll that isolation, anxieties about families left without support, deprivation of familiar comforts, and various indignities took on the prisoners. This was true whether they were Turkish officers or the poor, uneducated Syrian sailors he came to know so well. Hakim Nusrat Husain in his last days worried constantly about his aged parents, whose only son he was, his young wife, and their two children. Maulana Mahmudul Hasan had left his family in the care of a trusted Deobandi elder, but he felt deeply the indignity of placing this burden on him that now had stretched on so long. Uncertainty took a great toll on the prisoners.

Maulana Husain Ahmad in his memoir never spoke of his own losses, but in a letter to one of his elders he noted the tragedies that befell his family in the course of the war. His biographer, Muhammad Miyan, compared this reticence to the silences of the Companions of the Prophet about the suffering they endured in the Meccan period (M. Miyan 2005: 101). The Turks in Medina, facing the Sharif's revolt, arrested Husain Ahmad's father and his two brothers, Sayyid Ahmad and Mahmud Ahmad, as British subjects, and transported them to Turkey along with other Indians and Arab supporters of the British. Habibullah, Husain Ahmad's father, died in Adrianople. This blow was the greater since Habibullah's cherished hope in emigrating to Medina had been to be buried in the Prophet Muhammad's own city. The women and children left behind in Medina were not only bereft of male support but suffered the deprivations caused by the British blockade. Husain Ahmad's stepmother, his wife, his eighteen-month-old son Ashfaq Ahmad, and Syed Ahmad's wife and daughter all died (Madani 1951: II, 73). Left in Medina were only his own ten-year-old daughter Zohra, and Mahmud Ahmad's wife, who, after great difficulties, reached Adrianople. On the return journey to Medina, while traveling through Syria, little Zohra would die as well.

It was a collection of letters, for whatever reason accumulated and delivered together, which at one moment delivered all these blows. Wahid Ahmad, Husain Ahmad's nephew, would later recount the events of the terrible day when the news came. It was he who delivered the mail to his uncle, who was engaged as usual in the late afternoon in memorizing the Qur'an. Perhaps somehow apprehensive, Husain Ahmad immediately closed the Qur'an and opened the letters. As he read each letter, his face grew increasingly pale, and when he finished he quietly repeated the Qur'anic verse appropriate to news of a death, "We belong to God, and to God we will return." He then returned to his memorization, absorbed as he had been ten minutes earlier. Wahid Ahmad stood waiting anxiously for news of his loved ones. But, Wahid Ahmad would later reflect, with what words could his uncle have reported the news that "those dear and beloved beings, news of whose well being you await, are gone forever, and the family home you long to hear about has been uprooted for its eternal home" (Muhammad Husaini 2003: 86)?

Husain Ahmad recognized, as many would do after this war, the terrible impact of war on those who fought it and those who were caught up in it. He witnessed many suicides on Malta, many others lost to various forms of what he called "madness." Mr. Sidar, the poor Bengali, who shared no language with his fellow Indians except a bit of English with the Hakim, was one of those whose sanity was lost. Nothing against him had ever been proven (*Asir-i malta*: 137).

The cost of internment was enormous, not least for people like the Indians who were neither part of any enemy military nor convicted of any crime. This was the case even in such relatively benign conditions as the camp at Malta. Husain Ahmad, a mature person, was able, in fact, to use the prison experience for many of the activities he cherished most, not least devoted service to Maulana Mahmudul Hasan. Still, he would emerge from these years with an anti-colonial political critique shaped by his own painful, personal experiences of the injustice of these years, as well as by acute observation of the larger events of the day.

EVERYDAY ROUTINES: MUTUAL BONDS, COMMON COMMITMENTS

Husain Ahmad commented at one point that anyone seeing the group of five Indians would think they were a family, given their closeness and the fact that they spanned three distinct generations (*Asir-i malta*: 97). Husain Ahmad and Wahid, of course, were in fact biological family. It was Husain Ahmad and his father who had embraced the orphaned boy, making the difficult decision, for example, that he should leave his Turkish school in Medina, where they feared he was acquiring distaste for religion "in the European fashion" (*Naqsh-i hayat*: I, 127–128). Maulana Husain Ahmad took him to enroll at Deoband in 1913, whence Wahid had just returned with Maulana Mahmudul Hasan for a visit at the time of the arrest. The bonds of devotion on the part of the others to Maulana Mahmudul Hasan were of course also abiding and deep.

All were concerned with following the injunctions of the *shari'a* in their everyday life. For Maulana Mahmudul Hasan, for example, there was an undeviating commitment to the supererogatory prayers in the middle of the night, no matter his weakness, no matter the cold, no matter the care he had to take not to disturb the others, even during the first weeks of winter living in tents. The group would not eat improperly slaughtered meat, and ultimately worked out the strategy of selling the meat they received from the camp to "infidels." With the proceeds, they purchased other food and they received permission to bring small animals such as chickens into the camp that they would prepare themselves. They knew that other Muslims, especially modernists in India, favored eating meat slaughtered by

Christians or Jews (or automated machines) or argued that restrictions should be lifted during travel or other difficult circumstances. Husain Ahmad devoted several pages in his account of the Malta detention to showing each of these arguments to be fatuous. He even asked the question whether the Christians of today, given their irreligiosity and behavior, could be characterized as "people of the book" (*Asir-i malta*: 129–131).

Maulana Mahmudul Hasan also, as befits a Sufi elder, encouraged hospitality. The group welcomed their Syrian servant and other guests at meals. They never accepted shares of the Red Crescent parcels, and even contributed to a fund organized by the Turkish officers for those in need. Husain Ahmad basically took responsibility for the practical side of life and even took charge of the cooking. He measured their limited resources frugally, pressed for the transfer of the cash taken from them in Jeddah, and arranged for loans. To live on the financial edge was apparently Maulana Mahmudul Hasan's custom, even in India, where he sold off property, borrowed, and was always in debt (*Asir-i malta*: 145–146).

Their day was marked by the canonical prayers, inspection, food preparation, outings, and visits with other prisoners, including the Turkish officers whom they admired. This schedule allowed considerable time for their own projects. "This was a real college for learning," Maulana Husain Ahmad wrote, since no work was required by the authorities, books could be requested from outside, and other people had languages or skills they were prepared to teach (*Asir-i malta*: 131).

Maulana Mahmudul Hasan devoted himself to worship and meditation as well as to two major scholarly projects, a translation of the Qur'an and a commentary on the *hadith* collection of Bukhari. Both Husain Ahmad and 'Uzair Gul aided him in these projects. He also gave lessons to young Wahid Ahmad, whose education at Deoband had been so dramatically cut off by the internment. Like the poor Turk condemned to die, whose grave Maulana Mahmudul Hasan would visit, many in the camp were drawn to Maulana Mahmudul Hasan's holiness. Both the Turks and Europeans would call, particularly on the

'Id holiday, when they would present flowers, and even the English officers, according to Maulana Husain Ahmad, would lift their hats and even bow to him. "Truth and spirituality," Maulana Husain Ahmad wrote, "is such a thing that its impact surely takes effect" (*Asir-i malta*: 133). Among the Syrian sailors were several who actually took Sufi initiation from Maulana Mahmudul Hasan. Some gave up the camp meat and began to wear beards. The Indians also undertook to teach them to read and write. Maulana Mahmudul Hasan had declined the offer of better housing precisely because he did not want to be cut off from "ordinary people" (*Asir-i malta*: 154–155).

Husain Ahmad summed up Maulana Mahmudul Hasan's time on Malta as fulfillment of a divine plan quite apart from what the British thought they were doing:

> In short the truth of the matter is that Maulana Mahmudul Hasan in his whole life had never had such an opportunity for spiritual work, inner progress, and intimacy with his True Beloved like the days of his stay on Malta . . . It was a true gift from God for achieving the stages of inner progress. The Eternal Writer made this journey and this imprisonment the means for achieving those stages he had fixed for him from eternity. And once achieved, he sent him to his homeland and then summoned him [*Asir-i malta*: 160–161].

As for the others, Maulana Husain Ahmad saw everyone's accomplishments, including his own, with a somewhat critical eye.

'Uzair Gul set out to learn various Sufi disciplines from Maulana Mahmudul Hasan, who, apparently, was very fond of him and acted very informally with him. 'Uzair Gul was anything but assiduous. He gave up on his project to learn English and made little headway in memorizing the Qur'an. Ever convivial, he did learn Turkish well. As for the young Wahid Ahmad, the Turkish school in fact seems to have worked its influence on him, since his main interests seem to have been more worldly than spiritual. He plunged into learning French and German and, when he saw that the fortunes of war were turning, English as well. He did not get very far with his lessons on *hadith* and Qur'anic commentary.

As for Maulana Husain Ahmad himself, he describes himself as setting out three goals for himself during this period: to learn Turkish, to memorize the Qur'an, and to cultivate his "inner flame" (*batini ishti'al*). Memorizing the Qur'an had been a dream since his school days, periodically started and then stopped. Now, at last, he succeeded. He also made progress with Turkish. As hard on himself as he was on others, he wrote, however, that "despite the presence of a perfect *shaikh* and plenty of time," he made little progress in the third project (though, arguably, this was an area where modesty would not allow him to claim achievement in any case) (*Asir-i malta*: 191–193). Although Turkish would, in the end, prove of little use in his subsequent career in India, Maulana Husain Ahmad's choice of that language perhaps points to the public activism he would soon embrace.

COLONIAL INTERNMENT AS A SCHOOL FOR ANTI-COLONIALISM

Several dimensions of the experience of internment shaped and intensified the anti-colonialism of the Indian prisoners. First, there was to them evidence of injustice on every side, not least the coup in Arabia that had led to their arrests in the first place. The revolt was the prelude to even greater machinations on the part of Europeans, conducted in such decisive negotiations as the secret Sykes–Picot Agreement of 1916, noted above, which anticipated the carving up of the Middle East into spheres of British and French control at the end of the war with an arrogance and confidence that in retrospect seem inconceivable. That the Indian *'ulama* supported the forward-looking Turks and opposed the aristocratic Sharif and his European backers makes clear that their orientation was not "anti-modern," as Muslim opposition to Europeans (and, today, Americans) is so often taken to be, but political.

In Malta, as Husain Ahmad wrote, "every last person . . . was an enemy of the British government and the English state." And, he might have added, if they were not so before arriving, they would have been after. "If there was news of an English defeat or of some trouble befalling them or their clients, we rejoiced and raised flags and cheered. And if, God forbid, some bad news happened to Germany, Turkey, Austria, or Bulgaria, every last person looked sorrowful" (*Asir-i malta*: 132). The prisoners were allowed to receive newspapers, including *The Times* of London, *Le Matin* from Paris, an Italian paper, and both *Al-Ahram* and *al-Maqam* from Egypt. These were translated into different languages, with responsibility for the translation given to someone chosen by each group. Then, too, there would be new arrivals with their news. When Husain Ahmad and the others first arrived at the camp, exhausted, they were surrounded by people longing for news and, in the end, they were up most of that first night. The camp offered an unparalleled opportunity for discussing political matters, national histories, and, especially, politics of the present, Husain Ahmad noted, with no fear of the CID, nor any concern for government displeasure, so that people talked openly about their opinions (*Asir-i malta*: 128–138).

From the experience of Malta, Husain Ahmad took many lessons. He was exposed to the nationalist vision of other countries, especially heightened in a period of war. He experienced, as he had in Arabia, others' view of himself as "Indian," an experience he shared with Gandhi and other nationalists whose national identity crystallized abroad, where the sub-national identities so emphasized in India were insignificant. Indeed, the comparison with Gandhi, Husain Ahmad's senior by a decade, is striking. Each lived outside India for roughly two decades before returning to India in their forties. Both Gandhi and Husain Ahmad in their time abroad gained experience in working with people of all religious backgrounds in a common cause. About Malta, Husain Ahmad wrote:

> Among these three thousand, some were Muslims, some Christians, some Jews, some Catholics; some were black, some white; some eastern, some western; some civilian and some military, some Asians, some Africans, some Europeans, some Turkish. But trouble joined all in such a bond that each was ready to sacrifice his life, and in his heart

everyone breathed well-being for the other. This was an extraordinary vision, as if the differences of religion, nation, and homeland had completely disappeared from the human world . . . as if each was the other's real brother . . . Everyone viewed the English officers and soldiers with real anger, but looked at each prisoner with an eye of dignity and respect . . . [*Asir-i malta*: 132].

Every criminal detention provides an occasion for some kind of education, but rarely the education the authorities intended.

And the detention of Maulana Husain Ahmad and the others was long. With the armistice of November 11, 1918, rumors about release had begun to swirl, and shortly afterward prisoners began to leave the island. Husain Ahmad's published letters from this time (dated from November 5, 1918, to February 28, 1920) begin with high hopes of release and end with the sober news that Husain Ahmad and his companions, sixteen months later, were among the handful – perhaps twenty – of prisoners still left (Madani 1951 (hereafter *Maktubat*): II, 71–79). The delay in granting the release was owed to considerable debate among a range of officials in India and London, with the former, interestingly, urging release much sooner. The fear in London was that the "undesirable Indians," as they were initially called at the time of deportation – now "the dangerous Muhammadan malcontents" or "Indian Moslem agitators" – were likely to inflame public opinion, already negative, against the terms of the peace settlement with Turkey at a time when post-war discontent in India was simmering. The four surviving prisoners, insisting there was no case against them, petitioned the Secretary of State for India in May 1919 for release to "their own country"; and the Indian Khilafat Delegation in the following April took a complaint about the continued detention to London itself. Since the beginning of 1918, the Government of India had in fact secretly urged their release, arguing that detention was far more harmful than release, and pointing out, ironically, in relation to Maulana Mahmudul Hasan, their chief suspect throughout, that "hitherto he ha[d] not been a publicist or a political agitator" at all.

Finally, with the closure of the camp, arrangements were made for the four to leave. Husain Ahmad left Malta a different person than he had arrived. But what he took from his time on Malta, and the use he put it to thereafter, depended critically on his earlier experience that had made him the disciplined and focused Islamic scholar that he had by then become.

3

FLASHBACK: BECOMING AN ISLAMIC SCHOLAR IN COLONIAL INDIA AND MEDINA

At the time of his arrest in 1916, Maulana Husain Ahmad Madani was the very model of a modern Indian Islamic scholar. He was credentialed by graduation from one of the new, formally organized seminaries of the day. He had, in Maulana Rashid Ahmad Gangohi and, through him, Hajji Imdadullah, links to a luminous spiritual lineage. And he was firmly identified, as a Deobandi, with one of the sectarian orientations of Sunni Islam increasingly salient at the turn of the twentieth century for the Urdu-speaking Muslim elite. He had, moreover, attracted an international student following to his lessons in *hadith* in the holy city of Medina itself. Together, the distinctions Maulana Husain Ahmad embodied marked off Indian Islam from Islam elsewhere: its rigorous tradition of study of *hadith*; the integration of Sufism and scholarship; and the proliferation of sectarian orientations that made for a pluralism of interpretation and standards of authority.

The new seminaries, like the Darul 'Ulum at Deoband, offered a route to Islamic learning and authority for students of any background at no cost. Husain Ahmad and his brothers, for example, did not come from a wealthy or scholarly family. They were, however, accepted (though not without some controversy) as being of *"sayyid"* lineage and thus descendants of the Prophet Muhammad. They were also respected as a family that (newly) emphasized descent from great Sufi figures of the past. The old criteria for authority had thus not wholly given way to the prestige that came from individual attainment.

THE FAMILY

When Husain Ahmad set out to write the story of his life in the early 1940s, true to the conventions of Urdu biographical writing, he began by tracing his family genealogy. A conventional beginning it may have been, but Husain Ahmad deeply valued his rootedness in family relationships, his ties to his home area, and his appreciation of the family heritage of Sufism. His ancestors, he wrote, had first settled in the area of the eastern United Provinces in the early sixteenth century in the same place that he had spent his childhood, the country town of Tanda and its adjoining villages, in what had become in the eighteenth century the Mughal successor state of Awadh or Oudh. Husain Ahmad had no knowledge of where the family had come from before settling there, but since the first settler traced his Sufi lineage to one of the great holy men who flourished in Delhi at the turn of the thirteenth century, his ancestral lineage had apparently been based in the northern Gangetic plain for more than half a millennium (*Naqsh-i hayat*: I, 7–10).

Maulana Husain Ahmad made clear that his was a landowning, elite family, patronized in due course by the Mughals. As for whether or not the family was *sayyid*, in a letter to some inquirers, concerned that others were denying him that status, he wrote:

> I myself don't write "Sayyid" with my name since salvation depends on acts, not relationship. If a person has high rank but bad deeds, then, like the son of Noah, he is expelled from the lord's house. If someone is of low (*chamar* or *bhangi*) descent, and is a devout Muslim, his state of comfort is like that of [former slaves close to the Prophet] Bilal and Sohaib [*Maktubat*: I, 8].

Having redefined "*sayyid*" as dependent on behavior, not just lineage, he then concluded "My deeds do not give me permission to make such claims I am ashamed to say." He made explicit that the requisite deeds were service to the community (*umma*) and respect for all Muslims, no matter how poor, ignorant, or lowly (*choti zat*). That said, he did point out that his family had been resident in the same place for some 400 years, that their marriages were in fact with *sayyids* and well-born *shaikhs* (putative descendants of the Prophet's Companions), and that anyone who wanted to could make their own investigations (*Maktubat*: I, 8).

In his account, Maulana Husain Ahmad gave far more attention to another lineage: that of the Sufi initiation transmitted within his family whose chain led to Khawaja Muinuddin Chisti's chief disciple, Khawaja Qutbuddin Bakhtiyar Kaki (d.1235) (*Naqsh-i hayat*: I, 10–16). Both his family and their Sufism were deeply rooted in his home area and shared profoundly in the cultural forms of their Hindu neighbors. Bringing the story to the present, Husain Ahmad included in his autobiography examples of his own father's devotional verse, written not only in Persian and Urdu but in the local linguistic variant or *bhaka,* and in the form of *bhajans* shared with Hindu devotional songs (*Naqsh-i hayat*: I, 37–39).

But the family story also made clear that Maulana Husain Ahmad did not imagine some undifferentiated, "syncretic" or blended culture that did not distinguish separate distinctive traditions of symbols and institutions. Husain Ahmad, rather, told the story of his ancestor's arrival in terms of a distinctive Islamic presence coupled with a faith that divine intervention, mediated through Sufi charisma, favored Islam. When the ancestor, Shah Nurul Haqq, and other Muslims were, he said, tormented by the ruling Rajput clan, the Shah invited the *raja* to accept Islam and, when he refused, the Shah's miraculous *karamat* drove him from the fort (*Naqsh-i hayat*: I, 9–10).

By the time of Husain Ahmad's birth in 1877 the family's status, both worldly and spiritual, had fallen. Their land holdings had been severely reduced both by bad management and by usurpation. Only two decades earlier, their district, Faizabad, had been an area of extensive civil unrest during the so-called "Mutiny" of 1857. The motives for "disloyalty" in that uprising had been complex, and more than one figure had taken sides for contingent reasons of place and dependency as much as for any abstract commitment to one side or another. Many indeed had changed sides more than once. In Awadh, the British post-Mutiny solution had been to bolster large landlords who were regarded as "loyal" with rights to land and security of status that would, presumably, tie their interests to colonial interests and forestall future disorder. The arrangement served the British well, if not improving the well-being of subordinates and peasants. A class of powerful magnates, the "taluqdars," was set in place as a reliable collaborating class.

Husain Ahmad's family, by contrast, emerged from these years impoverished. The accidental death of his maternal grandfather, coupled with rumors that the family had sided with the rebels, seems to have given a local *raja*, an old enemy, a chance to usurp most of the family lands. In the disturbances of the civil unrest, all the family goods, including valuable documents, were plundered (*Naqsh-i hayat*: I, 24–25). Husain Ahmad's father, Habibullah (b. 1852), was orphaned, and, with no male adult left in the family, his aunt supported the child with earnings from spinning cotton (Goyal 2004: 19).

Habibullah attended the local colonial middle school and upon graduation became a teacher at a nearby primary school. He subsequently passed the "normal school" requirement, and became a headmaster in Bangarmao, in the district of Unao, where Husain Ahmad, the third of his five sons, was born. Shortly thereafter, Habibullah secured a transfer to his home town, where Husain Ahmad and his brothers would, in turn, study in the local government school, in Husain Ahmad's case up to age twelve.

In an act that would be decisive for the family's future, Habibullah, whose poetic verses are noted above, sought Sufi initiation, as did his wife, at the hand of one of the great spiritual guides of his day, Maulana Fazlur Rahman Ganjmuradabadi (1793–1895), a disciple of the great Delhi reformists linked to Shah Waliullah (1702–1763). The stimulus may well have come from Husain Ahmad's mother, whose own pious and learned mother had educated her and shaped her bent to Sufism. Their actions ended the break in the family's long tradition of producing Sufi adepts, since, for three or so generations, as Husain Ahmad writes, the family had produced only "worldly *zamindars* (landholders)" (*Naqsh-i hayat*: I, 76). The decision to become Ganjmuradabadi's disciples both aligned the family with the sectarian orientation of the *madrasa* at Deoband and shaped what would be an ever-increasing devotion to the Prophet. Habibullah was known as a man of extraordinary self-discipline, a recipient of revelations (*kashf*), and with an ability to heal (through taking on himself, and subduing, illness) as well as to effect other interventions on behalf of those in need. As for Husain Ahmad's mother, despite being burdened by the obligations of a large family and the demands of straitened circumstances, in Medina in particular, she was apparently unwavering in her Sufi devotions (*Naqsh-i hayat*: I, 34–40).

Within the household, Husain Ahmad's mother (1857/8–1904/5) was central to her children's informal education. It was another woman, Husain Ahmad's paternal great aunt, who had identified his mother as a bride precisely because she had been nurtured in Urdu and Hindi by her own competent mother. Her family claimed *sayyid* descent with a lineage that joined his father's six generations back. Husain Ahmad's maternal grandmother was known for receiving messages from the dead (*kashf-i qubur*). She had been instructed in Sufism by her maternal uncle and, in turn, taught her daughter not only explicitly religious texts but such vernacular love stories (*prem kahani*) as *Hans Jawahar* and *Padmawat*, the latter a Sufi mystic treatise in the guise of a Rajput romance focused on the quest for the beauteous Padmavat. These stories were rooted in epics and folk tales of the region, but they were given an allegoric gloss as stories of the human soul's love for the Divine. Husain Ahmad's mother inspired her children with her teachings and tales (*Naqsh-i hayat*: I, 27).

EVERYDAY LIFE AND EDUCATION IN TANDA

The family home town of Tanda is located on the Ghagra River in a region known for its rich agricultural lands. Crossed with waterways, particularly in its rainy season it is a place of luxuriant foliage and beauty. It also is a place of rich historical memory. The district town, Faizabad, was the first capital of the Awadh *nawwabs* in the late eighteenth century. It still boasts its elegant *nawwabi* buildings, including the *imambaras* built to perform the mourning rituals of the Shi'a sect, to which the *nawwabs* belonged, as well as the tombs of the royal women. Across the river from Faizabad is the Hindu pilgrimage town of Ayodhya, graced in Husain Ahmad's day with one of the earliest Mughal mosques, the Babari Masjid. It is a sad irony that Husain Ahmad, who so fervently believed that Muslims and Hindus would work together harmoniously in independent India, grew up near the site that by the late twentieth century was the epicenter of virulent anti-Muslim Hindu nationalism. In 1992 the mosque was torn down by Hindu activists who had launched a campaign to build a temple on what they claimed was the birthplace of the god Ram.

As for Tanda, then, as now, it was renowned as a center for excellent spinning and weaving. At the turn of the twentieth century, the population of about 20,000 had slightly more Muslims than Hindus. The town was an important marketing center. But it was also a place of holy sites and festivals: the shrine of a fourteenth-century holy man; an *imambara* where effigies were buried during the Muharram observances; a masonry platform in honor of Saiyyid Salar Mas'ud Ghazi, an enormously popular saint among both Hindus and Muslims. At the annual Hindu festivals of Ramlila, Ramnaumi, and the full moon of Kartik, thousands would assemble to bathe in the Ghagra (Nevill 1905: 270–273). Husain Ahmad's life-long assumption that Hindus and Muslims could live together was surely in part based on his own childhood experience of a society where both Hindus and Muslims interacted in many ways.

By the end of the century, Tanda had the classic institutions of local colonial rule: a police station, a post and telegraph office, a dispensary, and the vernacular middle school the boys attended. Husain Ahmad as a child may never have seen an Englishman, but his home area provided him with an enduring example of the costs of colonial rule. The poverty of the peasantry, linked in part to the "sub-infeudation" that British land settlement patterns encouraged, was particularly acute here. The district was racked by lawsuits over land in the late nineteenth century, a fruitless undertaking that only led to more indebtedness, as it did in Husain Ahmad's own family in these years. The instability that came from cash crops like indigo, and later sugar, was also evident in periods of late nineteenth-century famine, as was the severe inflation at the end of the century produced by British monetary policy (Nevill 1905: 21–37). Husain Ahmad's formal education was one thing; this informal experience of a society disadvantageous to his family and many others without question shaped him in decisive ways as well.

THE FORMATION OF AN ISLAMIC SCHOLAR

Habibullah's overriding goal in relation to his sons was to secure for them the classic Islamic education that he himself had never had. Habibullah's ambivalence toward his own colonial education was brought home to him by an ominous dream, recorded by Husain Ahmad, that his hands were covered in excrement at the prospect of learning English, required for advancement in his career (*Naqsh-i hayat*: I, 26). Husain Ahmad recalled his father once summoning all his sons and saying to them that he had nurtured them for only one reason: that they exert themselves (*jihad*) in the path of Allah and attain death (*shahadat*) in that cause (*Naqsh-i hayat*: I, 34). On the fringes of colonial society himself, Habibullah increasingly sought to create a world for his family in which goals, attainments, and respect were defined apart from colonial culture.

All five sons did indeed complete seminary education. Husain Ahmad's two elder brothers had, apparently, come first in the exams for the entire province in their final year at the government middle school, but rather than continue in the colonial system they both enrolled at the Darul 'Ulum at Deoband. The eldest, Siddiq Ahmad, who had differed with his father enough to leave home before going to Deoband, in fact upon completion of his studies took a position in the colonial education department. Nonetheless, he accompanied the family to Medina and primarily managed the family finances and business there until his untimely death at an early age (Goyal 2004: 21). A second brother who died young also opted for a secular career. Of the others, however, Husain Ahmad was engaged life-long in teaching and, in his final three decades, leading a *madrasa*; Saiyyid Ahmad founded a long-lived *madrasa* in Medina; and Mahmud Ahmad served as a *qazi* for many years in the Hijaz before shifting his activities to trade (*Naqsh-i hayat*: I, 29–31).

The boys were tutored from early childhood in Persian and Arabic to lay a foundation for higher learning. Husain Ahmad's memory of his father's role in his education was above all the memory of restrictions. Habibullah would beat a child who opted for play over study or forgot his lessons, a routine Husain Ahmad faced at school as well. From his mother he learned basic grammar and Qur'an, studying at home in the early morning before "imprisonment," as he put it, in school till evening, only to come home to be imprisoned again. As he tells his own story, if Husain Ahmad had been left on his own, he would have slipped out to play whenever he thought he could get away with it. He recalled his regrets at missing out completely on kites, *galli danda*, and other childhood games. Apparently out of despair at keeping Husain Ahmad under control once his elder brothers were no longer at home, in 1891 Habibullah decided to send him to join them at the seminary at Deoband (*Naqsh-i hayat*: I, 42–43).

The town of Deoband, although some 350 miles distant, would have seemed familiar to the boys, with its winding streets, its market, and its walls and buildings made of the narrow baked bricks common in the towns of Faizabad as well. The school's pioneer effort to transmit Islamic knowledge by organizing staff and instruction on the model of British colonial schools was, by the end of the century, well established, and its early graduates, fanning out across the country, had created schools on the Deoband model widely. The goal of the school was to preserve Islamic teachings by creating of a class of formally trained and popularly supported 'ulama who would serve as prayer leaders, guardians and trustees of mosques and tombs, preachers, muftis, spiritual guides, writers, and publishers of religious works. The Deobandis were among those 'ulama who took advantage of the newly available lithographic presses that made it possible to disseminate sacred texts and vernacular materials at relatively little cost.

In the traditional distinction between the Islamic "rational" disciplines, those reflecting human ratiocination like grammar, logic, philosophy, jurisprudence, and so forth, on the one hand, and the "revealed sciences" of Qur'an and hadith, on the other, the Deobandis represented a shift in emphasis to the latter, and, as noted above, particularly to hadith. In this they followed their forebear, Shah Waliullah Dihlawi. The course at Deoband, however, basically included the comprehensive curriculum in the classic disciplines worked out in the eighteenth century, the so-called dars-i nizami, developed by the Lucknow-based 'ulama of Farangi Mahall. This has been the standard curriculum in most Sunni seminaries of modern India. The curriculum included works of Arabic grammar, etymology, and syntax; Arabic literature; logic, philosophy, law; jurisprudence, prophetic traditions, Qur'an, and theology. The Deobandis were firmly committed to the Hanafi legal tradition. Their distinctive pattern was to couple dissemination of Islamic guidance along with opposition to a range of customary practices surrounding life-cycle events and the tombs of holy men that were seen either to reflect extravagance and social ostentation or to elevate holy men, the Shi'i imams, and the Prophet himself unduly (Metcalf 2002).

The deep bonds of male sociality that characterized the relationships of like-minded 'ulama were nurtured from students' earliest days in the school. The ties Husain Ahmad forged in his school days, in many cases, proved life-long and served as a template for relationships he would later develop, much as Husain Ahmad's family relationships had prepared him for submission to the authority of elders as well as responsibility for those younger. Students were often incorporated into the families of the teachers in those early days before more formal boarding arrangements were set up (*Naqsh-i hayat*: I, 44–48). Although Husain Ahmad received his meals from the home of Maulana Hafiz Muhammad Ahmad, it was toward Mahmudul Hasan and his family that he primarily turned:

> I took up residence with my brothers in a room near the home of
> Maulana Mahmud Hasan . . . My elder brother asked him [to initiate
> my studies] as a blessing . . . and he directed Maulana Khalil Ahmad
> Sahib to do so . . . Although I was then in my twelfth year, I was very
> small . . . and because a boy so small, from such a distance, was
> unusual, I was treated with great kindness . . . I would go to my
> teachers' houses to help with writing and accounts . . . and received
> great kindness from the wife of Maulana Mahmudul Hasan in
> particular [*Naqsh-i hayat*: I, 44].

At Deoband, Husain Ahmad, as he rather poignantly tells us, found his intellectual talents fostered and his inclinations shaped toward the school's centrally important emphasis on *hadith*. He also developed pride in his "alma mater":

> I never had much enthusiasm for study and would not study thoroughly
> or do much to review my books . . . As far as the beginning books, on
> which there was only an oral exam, I did well, but not so well in the
> later written ones . . . failing three of six in the first year . . . The night
> before the exam I would study the whole book and sleep only an hour
> or less. To stay awake I would prepare salty tea and whenever I felt
> sleepy, drink the tea and thus keep off the sleepiness for an hour or
> two. For I always needed much sleep and I especially feel sleepy when
> reading . . . After my first failure, praise God, I did not fail again, and
> within my class I often attained distinguished marks . . . Darul 'Ulum
> Deoband's exams, from the beginning, were made difficult, whether
> oral or written . . . When a student of the Darul 'Ulum entered
> government institutions (for the *maulavi fazil, maulavi 'alim* degree,
> etc.), or did exams after completing English classes, they were always

> most distinguished . . . Although I was always unenthusiastic and
> shrank from work and sacrifice, thank God gradually both my
> intellectual inclination and balance of character grew. At the very
> beginning my interest was in logic and philosophy, then in literature
> . . . then *hadith*, and the first two interests declined [*Naqsh-i hayat*:
> I, 46–48].

Husain Ahmad's self-presentation as a child who had to be shaped
into proper form conveys a certain humility. It is not unlike the picture of his childhood drawn by Husain Ahmad's close friend of a
slightly younger generation, Maulana Zakariyya Kandhlawi
(1885–1982), who recounts many episodes of paternal discipline to
tame his natural disposition in the direction of study and self-
sacrifice. In Husain Ahmad's case such a self-presentation may go
beyond convention (Metcalf 2004: 118). It may help explain and justify his later career, which was one far more of action than of scholarly production even while he never wavered from his commitment
to traditionalist Islamic knowledge.

On November 10, 1895, Maulana Fazlur Rahman
Ganjmuradabadi died at the advanced age of 105 years, leaving
behind, among his heartbroken disciples, Husain Ahmad's parents.
At the time of this death, Habibullah had not been named a successor
to Ganjmuradabadi, but in a subsequent dream he received *khilafat*
and *ijazat*, making him a successor who could initiate his own disciples. At this time of profound sorrow, Husain Ahmad's brother,
Sayyid Ahmad, wrote a letter urging his grief-stricken father to go
and settle in Medina. The letter, coming when it did, Husain Ahmad
wrote, set such a fire of love for the Prophet in his father's heart that
it was as if a match had touched alcohol. From then on, his passion
was to leave for Medina with a vision of making a permanent migration, in Islamic terms, a *hijrat*. He expected his sons to stay in Medina
as long as he was alive, but he retained a portion of his land in
Faizabad should the sons wish to return (*Naqsh-i hayat*: I, 32–34).

Husain Ahmad desperately wanted to stay behind in Deoband
to complete his final year of study. His in-laws, like his brothers',

similarly wanted their daughters to remain behind. Habibullah rather unrealistically said that if the girls did not want to go, they could get divorced. Husain Ahmad's own orphaned wife's uncle, who was employed in the great *taluqdari* estate of Balrampur, had suggested that she and Husain Ahmad settle with him in Lucknow, where he would arrange for Husain Ahmad to study Greco-Arabic medicine with the great doctor, Hakim 'Abdul 'Aziz. To this, Habibullah replied: "After having Husain Ahmad ride a horse, should I put him on a donkey? He will study religion, the best of education" (*Naqsh-i hayat*: I, 32–33, 49). Habibullah also directed both Husain Ahmad and Sayyid Ahmad to pledge allegiance to a Sufi guide, as Siddiq Ahmad had already done, before their departure to Medina, and both bound themselves at this point to Maulana Rashid Ahmad Gangohi.

In January of 1898, Habibullah's family departed for the Hijaz: the parents, five sons, one daughter, three daughters-in-law, and one grandchild. These were Muhammad Siddiq, his wife, and his son, Wahid Ahmad; Sayyid Ahmad and his wife; Husain Ahmad and his wife; Mahmud Ahmad; Riyaz Fatima; and Jamil Ahmad. It was not an easy trip. All western ports were closed that year on account of cholera. After ten days in quarantine in Allahabad, they traveled by heavily guarded train to the outskirts of Chittagong in Bengal where they spent something over a month in a *hajji* "camp," along with Bengalis, some Punjabis, and even travelers from Chinese Turkestan awaiting their ship for the Hijaz. They first reached Mecca, where they intended to wait for the fixed season to perform the *hajj*, and Husain Ahmad, as instructed by his own *shaikh*, Maulana Rashid Ahmad, was able to sit at the feet of Hajji Imdadullah, who had emigrated to Mecca when colonial suspicions fell on him after the uprising of 1857. Both Rashid Ahmad and Hajji Imdadullah were at the end of their lives, and Maulana Husain Ahmad was one of the youngest to have had a direct relationship to these exemplary holy men who were regarded as a source not only of guidance but of great charismatic power and blessing.

Four days out of Mecca, Husain Ahmad dozed off on camelback and had a dream that must capture the imagination of any scholar. In the dream, the Prophet Muhammad appeared, and Husain Ahmad fell at his feet. The Prophet raised up his head and said, "What do you wish?" Husain Ahmad replied, "That whatever books I have read, I may remember, and that those I have not read, I may have the capacity to understand." The Prophet answered, "I grant it." Cut off prematurely from his studies, Husain Ahmad was assured that his scholarly career had not ended (*Naqsh-i hayat*: I, 80). Even if his own inclinations had not been initially toward learning, he had come to share the value placed on scholarship by his elders.

In May of 1898 the family arrived, at last, in Medina. Husain Ahmad, now a young man of 21, effectively settled there, his stay broken only by travels, either for spiritual or family reasons, back to India: to Gangoh in 1901; to Deoband from 1909 to 1911, and finally to Deoband again in 1913. Family life in Medina was not easy. The women of the family themselves did the menial work that servants had helped with at home. After problems with rentals, the family was able to secure land and physically built their own home, with Husain Ahmad doing the lion's share (Goyal 2004: 44). At first, the family opened a small provisions shop, but within a year they abandoned that project as unprofitable. Husain Ahmad worked in the shop as long as the family had it, took up some work as a copyist, offered tuition to a handful of children, and, at the same time, struggled to complete the texts he would have studied at Deoband. Determined to be able to make a career as a teacher, he set out to gain mastery of spoken Arabic. He memorized Arabic texts to gain fluency in his lessons and struggled to complete the books he had left unfinished. As he later wrote, initially he was not diligent in his spiritual disciplines on account of all his other obligations.

THE SUFI PATH

In 1900 Maulana Rashid Ahmad Gangohi, perhaps aware of his disciple's preoccupations, perhaps sensing the short time left to him, wrote that he wished Husain Ahmad to be present with him in

Gangoh. Despite the family's difficulties, Husain Ahmad made the visit, accompanied by his eldest brother, Muhammad Siddiq, who seized the opportunity to go as well. It would be the last time they would see their *shaikh* alive. As Husain Ahmad described the trip, his brother went directly to Gangoh while he stopped for one day at Deoband and proceeded to Gangoh, some twenty-five miles distant, on foot. He wept as he proceeded, he wrote, thinking of his short-comings. Their *shaikh* welcomed them, presented them with cloth-ing, and had Maulana Muhammad Yahya Kandhlawi, who was with him in those days, ask if the brothers needed such help as finding employment: "I answered that I had no purpose but seeking the Essence of Truth" (*Naqsh-i hayat*: I, 87). Husain Ahmad followed the hospice's routines, including long periods of *zikr* repetition and meditation. He was instructed in what Maulana Rashid Ahmad called the summation of all the distinctive Sufi lineages or *silsila*. After forty days, Maulana Rashid Ahmad wrapped turbans on each of the brothers' heads (*Naqsh-i hayat*: I, 87). They thought that these were turbans simply honoring their accomplishments (*fazilat*) but they were in fact turbans of succession (*khilafat*). Husain Ahmad wrote that he "wept continuously, thinking of my lack of skill, of intention, of progress." He also received a dream interpreted to mean that he had also been granted permission by Hajji Imdadullah to make disciples as successor to him (*Naqsh-i hayat*: I, 86–89).

Some two months after his arrival, Husain Ahmad seems to have "cracked" under the intensity of this experience, feeling such pressure that he would be desperate to break off his meditations and run outside. Maulana Rashid Ahmad used the example of Hajji Imdadullah who periodically shared this experience and would then undertake a journey until he was restored. The two brothers set out for the Sabiri Chishti shrine at Kalyar. They also stopped at Deoband, both destinations within the same Saharanpur district as Gangoh. Shortly after their return, they departed for Medina, visiting Faizabad and Bhopal en route to join the *hajj* pil-grimage leaving from Purbandar in Gujarat. The trip had taken seven months.

Maulana Rashid Ahmad died in 1905, but Husain Ahmad's relationship to him persisted:

> After his death, however, I became more disciplined, and I practiced breathing exercises in the Prophet's mosque. As I did, I found that my love and the bond in my heart for Rashid Ahmad was growing intensely . . . thus it became even greater than my love and bond for Mahmudul Hasan, although that love did not diminish . . . I soon had many dreams of virtuous people and encounters (*ziyarat*) with [the Prophet]. I would go every night to the mosque that has the tomb of the Prophet . . . and on account of repeating *zikr*, my body would begin to move out of control . . . then, if other people were present, I would go outside to a deserted area . . . Once a powerful feeling came over me that my body had become Maulana Rashid Ahmad's body [*Naqsh-i hayat*: I, 80–81].

This was the state called *fana fi'sh shaikh*, annihilation in the *shaikh*, an experience understood to be a step toward the next step of "annihilation" in the Prophet and then, ideally, in the experience of the Divine itself.

Among the cherished dreams recorded by Husain Ahmad were many that came when he was facing some problem. Some eighteen that he recorded involved the Prophet, Abraham, and Rashid Ahmad giving him food such as dates, pumpkin seeds, sweets, or, most often, milk or buttermilk. In one he was lying under a green shawl in the Prophet's mosque and someone told him that his feet were like the Prophet's. He saw the Prophet in another dream granting him knowledge; in another he saw the Prophet and felt no gulf between him and himself. In dreams he received initiation from a dozen saints. He was assured of a relationship to the Caliph 'Usman. He was told that he would become an *imam*. He was promised that the Divine Grace once directed toward Mahmudul Hasan would now be directed toward him (*Naqsh-i hayat*: I, 90–97). Husain Ahmad's links to great spiritual elders played an inextricable part in his own life trajectory and in the status he was accorded.

A SECTARIAN CONFLICT

Upon his return to Medina from Gangoh in 1901, Husain Ahmad returned to his teaching, employed now in the seminary Shamsiyya Bagh as well as engaged with private pupils. Muhammad Siddiq was hired to teach the children of a newly arrived merchant from the Indian port of Surat. Maulana Husain Ahmad's teaching style, which he described as the style of the Khairabad 'ulama, was to prepare the text and commentary so thoroughly that he could teach without written materials. His circle of instruction grew and included students from a widespread geographic area. He taught long days, beginning after the pre-dawn prayer and continuing until night. Differences with the school officials, including their objection to his teaching pupils in the Prophet's Mosque free of charge, led him to resign his position at the school so that he could continue teaching privately (Goyal 2004: 41).

His remarkable teaching success, however, was soon put at risk by an episode thrust upon him by the sectarian debates that were taking new shape among Muslim scholars in India in the early twentieth century. The episode was troubling enough that, even writing his autobiography forty years later, Maulana Husain Ahmad included almost twenty pages of report and analysis devoted to the controversy (*Naqsh-i hayat*: I, 100–118).

Maulana Ahmad Riza Khan Barelwi (1856–1921) was a charismatic and prolific scholar based in the northern Indian town of Bareilly. In the late nineteenth century, he carved out an orientation among Sunni Muslims that came to represent, along with Deobandi teachings, one of the two major sectarian divides within Sunni Islam in India (Sanyal 2006). Outsiders called his followers "Barelwis"; they called themselves "Ahl-i Sunnat wa Jama'at," People of the Tradition and the Community, claiming to be the authentic inheritors of the Prophet's tradition. Like the Deobandis, the Barelwis specialized in disseminating and teaching what they considered authentic *hadith*. Both engaged in public and written debate with each other and other Muslim groups, as well as with the proselytizing Hindu Arya Samaj. Both issued advisory opinions, *fatawa*, widely. Generally speaking, the Barelwis were more open to accepting what the Deobandis considered false innovations in relation to holy men, the Shi'i *imams*, and the Prophet Muhammad. These included not only doctrinal issues but also devotional practices at shrines, the Muharram observances of the Shi'a, and such celebrations as that of the Prophet's birthday. The Barelwis insisted they alone showed the Prophet and other revered figures the deference they deserved. Although in the early years the Barelwis appear to have been a more rural population, the two orientations are difficult to distinguish sociologically.

Maulana Ahmad Riza's attack on the Deobandis focused on great classic theological debates that sought to strike a balance between the omnipotence of God and the singular achievements of his prophets and saints. In 1903, Ahmad Riza published his *Husamu'l-haramain 'ala a'naq ahl al-kufr wa'l main*, "The Sword of the Haramain at the Throat of the People of Kufr and Falsehood." To that point, Ahmad Riza had countered his opponents with debates, *fatawas* on specific points, refusal to pray with them, and argumentative written replies that piled citation upon citation. Now, however, he went so far as to label his opponents *kafir*, outside the bounds of Islam.

He attacked great Deobandis by name, and he labeled them "Wahhabi," then, as now, a term as much political as scientific and bound to alarm colonial authorities. He also targeted Mirza Ghulam Ahmad (1835–1908), founder of the Ahmadiyya movement, another sectarian orientation of the day that was taken to exalt its founder to prophetic status. This was a kind of guilt by association since Deobandis opposed Ghulam Ahmad's views as well. Put schematically, Maulana Muhammad Qasim Nanotawi was tarred with denying the uniqueness and finality of the Prophet because of his contention that God could create infinite worlds and prophets should he so wish. Maulana Rashid Ahmad was credited with holding that God was a liar, a similar distortion of the argument that no limit could be placed on what God could or could not do. Finally, Rashid Ahmad, with Maulana Ahmad Ambathawi and Maulana Ashraf 'Ali

Thanawi (1864–1943) were all said to have elevated Satan above the Prophet on the grounds that they denied the Prophet *'ilmu'l-ghaib*, "knowledge of the unknown," so that, presumably, on some points Satan could be better informed (Metcalf 2002: 307–11; Sanyal 1996: 230–40).

Sectarian debates of this sort were more exercises in group solidarity and loyalty than in intellectual exchange. They seem to have served as a way of generating popular followings for a religious leadership who depended on a popular base, not state patronage. On this occasion, as on others, stereotyped arguments were exchanged. Each side firmly believed itself to be showing forth true beliefs and perfect devotion to the Prophet. Each side always claimed victory. This debate, however, spilled outside the conventional form because in 1906 Ahmad Riza brought his pamphlet to the Hijaz and secured the signatures of very substantial numbers of *'ulama* who accepted – or, from the Deobandi point of view, were taken in by – his arguments.

Ahmad Riza's success was potentially devastating for Maulana Husain Ahmad, both personally and professionally. He therefore sought out signers, especially from families whose children he had taught, and, as he reports, he was able to convince them of the merit of his own and his elders' teachings. He also wrote a detailed refutation of Ahmad Riza's accusations, *al-Shihab al saaqib 'ala al mustariq al kaadhib*, "The Penetrating Flames for the Bogus Eavesdropper." Deobandis in India responded with *fatwas* of their own, collecting signatures supporting themselves from across India. Husain Ahmad's role on this occasion confirmed his maturity as a Deobandi scholar and enhanced his reputation both in the Hijaz and in India.

INDIA, 1909–1911 AND 1913

A few years later, Maulana Husain Ahmad again returned to India. The immediate occasion for this trip was to arrange a marriage following the death of his wife, who had passed away from tuberculosis, leaving behind a young daughter. Judging from the mortality rate in this one family, it was the typically unnamed women, at particular risk in childbearing, as well as children, who disproportionately suffered. Husain Ahmad's father had taken the position that neither the Arabian girls nor the assimilated daughters of Indian immigrants coped well with their Hindustani culture. From experience with two Arab daughters-in-law, they judged the local girls to have more extravagant tastes and an inclination to provide more hospitality than the family's limited means would permit. In Arabia, the family believed, it was also hard to find someone of the right social class (*kufw*) for a marriage.

Husain Ahmad was accompanied on this journey by the elderly Hajji Shaikh Ahmad 'Ali, a fellow disciple with Habibullah of Maulana Fazlur-Rahman Ganjmuradabadi. A man of great piety and simplicity, Ahmad 'Ali had founded a *madrasa* in a mosque in Faizabad, soon acquiring its own building and a highly competent Deoband-trained teacher. The two men performed the *hajj* and *umra* pilgrimages in Mecca and traveled together as far as Bombay and Jhansi, separating at that point to proceed to Faizabad and Deoband respectively. In Deoband, Maulana Husain Ahmad began contacting various relatives about a possible wife, while his father was busy writing letters from Medina. It turned out that no one was eager, as Husain Ahmad put it, to give one of their daughters only to have her taken off to Medina. The pull of the spiritual power of Medina apparently did not extend either to wishing to intermarry with the residents or, necessarily, to living there.

After six months, Maulana Husain Ahmad turned to outsiders, including an old family friend, Hafiz Zahid Hasan Amrohawi (later his faithful correspondent in Malta), whose kindness now would "exceed all bounds." It happened that Zahid Hasan had been asked by one Hakim Ghulam Ahmad, a disciple of Maulana Rashid Ahmad Gangohi, to keep his middle daughter in mind for a suitable marriage. Hakim Ghulam Ahmad agreed to the match provided, first, that the wedding would be contracted in the presence of the great teachers of Deoband and, second, that after a year or two, Husain

Ahmad would bring his daughter back to India for a visit. Maulana Mahmudul Hasan urged Husain Ahmad to agree. Scholarly and Sufi bonds, in the end, not family, secured the marital relationship that Husain Ahmad needed. To look ahead to the sad denouement of this connection, this was the wife who would die with her son in Medina during Maulana Husain Ahmad's internment in Malta, another son having died even earlier.

Maulana Husain Ahmad, as he describes this trip, had undertaken it happily so that he could go to Deoband directly and resume his studies. He immediately joined Maulana Mahmudul Hasan's classes in the *hadith* collections of Tirmidhi and Bukhari. Husain Ahmad lived in Mahmudul Hasan's household, first alone and then with his new wife, and accompanied Mahmudul Hasan if he traveled. He soon accepted a regular position as teacher at the school and participated, as described above, in the great convocation organized in 1910.

In 1911, Maulana Husain Ahmad returned to Medina, sailing from Bombay to Port Said and from there to Haifa, and thence on the new Hijaz Railway, on which students and scholars received free passage. In 1913, he was constrained to take his wife and infant son, Altaf Ahmad, back to India in keeping with the terms of his agreement. He used the occasion to take along his nephew, Wahid Ahmad (the only living offspring of his eldest brother, who had died the year earlier), in order to settle him for study in Deoband.

Although the previous trip had also been motivated by familial concerns, it had served Husain Ahmad's intellectual, personal, and professional interests well. This time the stay was brief, and consumed with family worries. The cherished child had been much admired aboard ship by women who concluded that his unusual beauty was a product of his birth in a holy place. Maulana Husain Ahmad believed that someone among these women had cast an evil eye upon the child. Little Altaf was sick during the whole trip and passed away shortly after the return to Medina (*Naqsh-i hayat*: I, 118–128). Such absorption in personal worries is a fit conclusion to this section since such anxieties would soon give way to new engagements and new concerns.

MAULANA HUSAIN AHMAD AT THIRTY-FIVE

As Maulana Husain Ahmed wrote the story of his life up to early middle age, he identified a series of critical moments when his elders set his natural bent in directions he would not have chosen. First, as a fun-loving child, he was shaped by an extraordinary discipline of long hours of study in which mastery of the great classical tradition of Islamic learning was central. Second, once at Deoband, he initially inclined toward subjects like philosophy and logic, but, thanks to the influence of his teachers, he soon found himself absorbed in the study of Prophetic traditions. Third, at the choice of his elders, and against his own inclination, he took initiation in his late teens at the hand of Maulana Rashid Ahmad Gangohi. And finally, at his father's insistence, he had to move to Medina and establish himself there. Maulana Husain Ahmad imagined his life as embedded in relationships of family, Sufi initiation, and scholarly networks. For him, the role of his elders in making him who he was was central. He held fast to their values, religious and in due course political, life-long. The parameters and values of his world, like his father's, were shaped in a cultural sphere apart from those of the colonial state. As a person, he appears even at an early age as someone persistent, optimistic, and responsible, qualities that must be weighed in analyzing the subsequent course of his life.

By thirty-five, Maulana Husain Ahmad was a person who had accepted substantial family obligations. He had faced great personal losses in the deaths of his mother, his eldest brother, his first wife, and two small sons. He had emerged as one of the leading figures of his generation of graduates of Deoband, someone known as a recipient of spiritual blessings and respected for his scholarly attainments. Overcoming great challenges, he had become a well-respected teacher in Medina, attracting to his circles not only Indian students but students from a wide range of Muslim populations. He contributed substantially to the family livelihood. In the *fatawa* crisis of 1906, he had shown himself able and willing to make an effective intellectual defense of the scholarly position and personal integrity

of the Deobandis, and he had secured the good-will of many of the
'ulama of Mecca and Medina because of their respect for his work.
The Indian-based Deobandis especially valued his fluent spoken
Arabic. He had even come to the point where he set some of his own
priorities, resisting, for example, his father's explicit wish that he
would continue his legacy of Sufi healing and similar interventions in
people's lives (*Naqsh-i hayat*: I, 34—35). Soon Husain Ahmad's priorities would be significantly enlarged with the onset of war,
Mahmudul Hasan's arrival, and his political education in Malta.

BECOMING A "NATIONALIST MUSLIM": INDIA IN THE 1920s

The detention in Malta had finally ended. On March 20, 1920, and only because of the closing of the camp, the long trip home began. The journey was a slow one, some three months of traveling, beginning with a quarantine camp in Alexandra. The British officials somewhat unsuccessfully tried to isolate the Indians, no easy task since they were overjoyed at finding Pathans manning the ship, Indian cooks and other employees working in the camp, and Turkish officers whom they were eager to meet as well. Then on to Suez, and finally, on June 8, 1920, Bombay. A joyous welcoming party of Mohandas Karamchand Gandhi (1869–1948), leading figures in the Khilafat Movement, and other Deobandis was waiting on the docks to greet them (*Asir-i Malta*: 203–205).

Maulana Husain Ahmad intended to accompany Maulana Mahmudul Hasan back to India. But it was not at all clear whether he would stay in India or return to his shattered family in Medina. This indecision may seem astonishing given the role that Husain Ahmad was to play in the nationalist movement virtually from the moment he stepped ashore. But while his political education in Malta had intensified his anti-colonialism, that was a cause he could pursue in Medina or elsewhere, and whatever he did politically, in any case, was always understood by him to be above all in the service of Islamic learning and Islamic practice.

Husain Ahmad's Indian ties were deep, to be sure, but his ties to the Hijaz and his two surviving brothers were deep as well. In the end, it was his bond to Maulana Mahmudul Hasan that proved critical in his decision. In the course of the trip, he agreed that he would stay in India because his revered elder said he needed him to aid in the completion of the *hadith* commentary that he had started during internment. This decision underlines the depth of his scholarly commitment and spiritual bonds at a time when his nationalism had not yet taken practical shape. In the end, he did not pursue the scholarly project at all, but almost immediately turned to the Islamic teaching and political activism within India that would subsequently fill his life.

Husain Ahmad would soon write to his former student, Maulana 'Abdul Haqq Madani (who had grown up in Medina as the son of an Indian doctor employed by the Turks) to explain his absence from Medina during the holy month:

> I long to be with you whether in Ramzan or "not-Ramzan," but what is most beloved has to be whatever is good for Muslims. And so I have preferred to live far away although my heart is distraught at thinking about Medina the Radiant, the Prophet, the residents of Medina, and my dear brothers [*Maktubat*: I, 20–21].

His commitment to Indian nationalism had become central to his commitment to Islam. This transition in his loyalty was shaped by circumstances in India that were far different from when he had last been there.

Now Husain Ahmad would "re-invent" himself in a new landscape of voluntary national organizations on the one hand and popularly oriented Islamic teaching and preaching on the other. He would, moreover, learn a new and effective rhetoric in the Indian political context, one that challenged the British on their own moral grounds and one that mastered the legitimate, but unrealized, rights of religious freedom, democracy, self-determination, and minority cultural protection that now resonated world-wide. Husain Ahmad's politics challenge assumptions that Islamic political actors are invariably rigid or trapped in some "medieval" past, even as they do not fit easily into contemporary definitions of liberal democracy.

BOMBAY, THE KHILAFAT MOVEMENT, AND POLITICAL AWAKENING

The decade of the 1910s in India had seen political life substantially shaped by events on the international scene. Muslim opinion was particularly alienated by Britain's unwillingness to defend the Ottoman Empire against Russia and against uprisings in the Balkans and Greece. Since the late nineteenth century, Muslims had debated the position of the Ottoman sultan as *khalifa* for all Muslims. Muslim loyalists to the colonial regime, for the most part, opposed this concept. Supporters, however, not only saw the caliph as a symbol of Muslim power that indirectly enhanced theirs, but also found in the caliphate an ideal to challenge colonial racism and imperialism. This attraction to the Ottoman caliphate was a modern development, the fruit of late nineteenth-century travel and communications, coupled with anxiety over European domination.

The position of the Ottoman caliph was an open question. Although Sunni Muslims agreed on the *khilafa*, or "succession" of the four "rightly-guided caliphs" who initially succeeded the Prophet Muhammad, there was no consensus that those who followed them had upheld the proper principles of succession. The caliphate was divided, at the mercy of warlords, and invoked more as an ideal than as any reality. The Delhi Sultans (Turks and Afghans who ruled much of India from the thirteenth to the fifteenth centuries) offered pro forma acknowledgement of the late Abbasid caliphs in Baghdad and Cairo. Even that was dropped by the Mughals who followed; they simply used the term to describe their own position of power. Only in the late eighteenth century did the Ottomans, ironically in the context of European negotiations, claim for themselves a universal "spiritual" sovereignty or *khilafa*.

The cause of the Ottomans and the caliphate was initially taken up by western-educated Indians like Muhammad 'Ali, Zafar 'Ali Khan, and Abdul Kalam Azad, all of whom were publishing Urdu-language newspapers at the beginning of the War. They were soon joined by a handful of *'ulama*, of whom the most important was Maulana 'Abdul

Bari of Lucknow. Active as well were Dr. M. A. Ansari and Hakim Ajmal Khan, who, as noted in Chapter 1 above, had supported a medical mission in the Balkan wars and an organization to aid pilgrims to the Holy Places, the Khuddam-i Kaaba. Maulana Husain Ahmad's testimony in Cairo in 1916 made clear the gap between the Deoband teachers and men like Muhammad 'Ali, the "men of the new light (Nai Roshani)" (PRO/TNA: FO 686/149/f.208. Foreign Office. Jeddah Agency. Papers. Silk Letter Case, 1916–1917).

What would move people like Maulana Husain Ahmad to now join with the modernist "men of the new light" in defense of what might seem a chimerical cause without historic tradition? In part, these Indians of very different backgrounds converged in their outrage at the arrogance of the European assumptions that the Middle East was theirs for carving up, even if masked under the vocabulary noted above of "progress and humanity" or "trusteeship." Lord Kitchener, the secretary of war, was among those, described in Chapter 2 above, who maneuvered to supplant the Turks in Arabia with the extraordinary argument that if Britain seized Arabic-speaking areas of the Ottoman Empire, they could then set up an alternative caliph and thus control all "Islam." Bedecked with the rhetoric of *soi-disant* experts, this theory claimed that Muslims would readily accept this new caliph on the grounds that only an Arab, ideally of the Prophet's tribe of Quresh, not a Turk in Istanbul, could be a "real" caliph. In his machinations to prop up the Sharif, Kitchener issued the following coy statement: "It may be that an Arab of true race will assume the Kalifate at Mecca or Medina, and so good may come by the help of God out of all the evil that is now occurring" (Fromkin 1990: 103–104). Now, in the post-war settlements, the Ottoman lands would be portioned among Europeans, and Palestine, as promised in the Balfour Declaration of 1916, opened up to Jewish settlement by the promise of British support for the Zionist dream of a Jewish homeland (Fromkin 1990: 42–43).

Meanwhile, there was a heightening of expectations within India that the conclusion of the war would bring the "self-determination" that the Allies claimed that they were fighting for. India had, as noted above, made extraordinary sacrifices for the war effort, with heavy troop deployment, levies on Indian revenues that had increased 10–15 percent each year, and the disruption of external markets. For the population as a whole this had been a time of acute economic distress. There were also draconian restrictions on civil rights during the war years, above all in the Defence of India Act, March 1915, and many internments, apart from those on Malta.

There had been every expectation in India that a new political era was about to dawn. The war years had seen alliances formed among moderate and radical nationalists, as well as between the Indian National Congress and the Muslim League, the party that shared the Congress nationalist vision of self-rule but had been formed in 1906 (at the time of the Bengal partition) specifically to speak for the presumed interests of Muslims. Particularly heartening had been the "Montagu Declaration" of 1917, confirming on the part of the Secretary of State for India the British government's intention to move toward "self-governing" institutions and ultimately "responsible government." These hopes were rudely dashed. The council reforms (the Montagu–Chelmsford Reforms), issued in 1919, far from offering self-government, provided only constrained autonomy at the provincial level. The restrictions on civil liberties were not withdrawn, but re-affirmed in the notorious Rowlatt Acts, under whose aegis one General Dyer, on April 13, 1919, opened fire on a peaceably assembled gathering in Amritsar in the Punjab, leaving hundreds dead and over a thousand wounded. Dyer never regretted his actions and, although relieved of duty in India, was welcomed as a hero in Britain.

In the momentous year of 1919, the All-India Khilafat Committee was formed by a wide range of Muslim leaders, angry and dismayed as the peace conference delivered large areas of the Middle East, including Muslim holy places, to puppet rulers. Following a meeting of the Khilafat Committee later that same year, the Jamiat Ulama-i-Hind (the Organization of Indian Ulama) emerged in order to give voice to specifically "religious" concerns of Muslim Indians. Meanwhile, Gandhi had returned after twenty years to his native

India from South Africa. There he had defended the interests of the Indian population and developed a powerful tool of peaceful protest, *satyagraha* ("truth force"), which he began to deploy in the interests of specific peasant and worker grievances within India at the end of the War. Gandhi, other Congress leaders, and the Khilafatists would soon come together. They shared a moral vision that deplored British exploitation and suppression of Indian rights as well as the British creation of a new domain of European imperialism in Muslim lands (Metcalf and Metcalf 2006: Chapter 5).

The first Khilafat Conference, held in Delhi in November 1919, was attended by Hindu leaders including Gandhi, Swami Shradhanand, Madan Mohan Malaviya, and Jawaharlal Nehru. The conference accepted, even before the Indian National Congress did so, Gandhi's proposal to boycott European goods, especially cloth in favor of hand-loomed *khadi*, as well as to withhold cooperation from government institutions – Gandhi's key tool of pressure (Minault 1982: 77–78). Gandhi insisted that his embrace of the *khilafat* cause was an act of "friendship" and not some kind of "deal" in which there was some exchange, some quid pro quo with Muslims; but the iden-tification of the *khilafat* with the larger nationalist movement in fact mobilized Muslims in large numbers to the nationalist cause. There were *'ulama* who did not support the *khilafat* movement, condemned by those who did as "loyalist," and there were secular politicians, most importantly Muhammad Ali Jinnah, for whom *'ulama* participation in politics was distasteful. The Khilafat cause and the Punjab outrages, however, formed the rallying cry of a new stage in Indian political life.

THE SHAIKHUL HIND, MAULANA MADANI, AND NON-COOPERATION

When the former prisoners arrived in Bombay two parties awaited them. On one side was the welcoming party. On the other, an English CID officer, accompanied by three Indians including, yet again, the ubiquitous Baha'uddin known from Jeddah, who escorted Maulana Mahmudul Hasan while still on board ship to meet Sir Rahim Bakhsh (1857–1935), Regent of the Muslim-ruled princely state of Bahawalpur (and soon to be an active political voice for the conservative interests of the princely rulers). He described himself to Maulana Mahmudul Hasan as someone who wished him well, and he urged him to avoid the assembled welcoming party, go directly to the train, and head straight for Deoband. There he could spend his old age in such a way that he would never again bring government suspicion upon himself. Rahim Bakhsh failed. The reason for his effort was clear – to keep the Maulana, as he saw it, from falling into the hands of the movement that was sweeping Muslims in India, the Khilafat Movement.

The Khilafat leaders served as hosts and organizers of meetings that would fill the few days that Maulana Mahmudul Hasan and his companions spent in Bombay. The Maulana declared his full support to the Khilafat program, including the program of non-cooperation that had been accepted in the previous year, attended a public meeting to welcome him, and spoke publicly (*Naqsh-i hayat*: II, 247). The Khilafat committee gave him the title "Shaikhul Hind," the Leader of India, a title by which he would subsequently be known. Barely a month after his return, the Shaikhul Hind issued a *fatwa* advising Muslims to withdraw from all government-supported schools and colleges, resign all government jobs, return all government titles, refrain from participating in the councils set up by the 1919 council reform act, and use only Indian-produced goods (*swadeshi*), of which *khadi* was the most visible symbol. While the specific points were those of Gandhi's program, the rationale was not: the Shaikhul Hind was explicit that the goal in following what might prove difficult steps would be "to serve the cause of Islam" even while they also asserted both Muslim and Hindu rights.

In the short time left to him, weak as he was, the Shaikhul Hind toured and spoke constantly for the nationalist cause. He attended the meeting at Aligarh Muslim University when students withdrew to establish the Jamia Millia Islamia, a new national university for

Muslims that would separate itself from government support and the loyalist tradition of Aligarh. In his address, the Shaikhul Hind spoke with admiration to "the children of this great nation" who had been educated in modern institutions yet were more active than the students of religious schools in the nationalist cause. Now in this new institution, he said, students would master modern knowledge, yet, free from government influence, be exposed to Islam as well (Muhammad Mian 2005: 63). He also addressed the second annual conference of the Jamiat Ulama, imploring religious leaders to remember that their enemy was the British and that they must preserve good relations with Hindus. In Delhi, he stayed with Dr. Ansari, who also provided his medical care. But on November 30, 1920, the Shaikhul Hind passed away and was laid to rest with great mourning in Deoband. Short as was his final time in India, he set the path that Maulana Husain Ahmad would follow. In India he was now "Maulana Madani," the *maulana* from Medina. Although Maulana Madani in his humility refused to allow anyone to speak of him as the Shaikhul Hind's successor, it was as such that he was widely regarded.

THE DOUBLE STRAND OF ACTIVISM: THE "KARACHI SEVEN" AND ISLAMIC RENEWAL

In the year that followed the Shaikhul Hind's death, it fell to Maulana Madani to be the authoritative Islamic voice that confirmed the Shaikhul Hind's widely supported *fatwa* in favor of non-cooperation. This was a period of great excitement, of expectation that self-government would come soon, and of cooperation between Congress and Khilafat. Maulana Madani attended Khilafat and Jamiat Ulama meetings in Calcutta and throughout rural Bengal; he came twice to the United Provinces and chaired a joint meeting of the Jamiat Ulama and Khilafat; and he spoke at a joint meeting organized by the Congress and the Khilafat Committee in Seohara (*Naqsh-i hayat*: II, 272–273). At every point he struck the same themes: the role of imperialism in undermining Islamic power; the British conquest of India as a tool in this destruction; the glorious economic and cultural past of India in contrast to the deplorable conditions of the present; and the need for Hindus and Muslims to struggle together for freedom.

In July 1921, at the Karachi session of the All-India Khilafat Committee, it was Maulana Madani, introduced by Muhammad 'Ali as "a true devotee of the late Shaikh-ul-Hind Maulana Mahmood-al-Hassan [and an internee] at Malta and Egypt," who proposed what would be the most notorious resolution of the occasion. This was a *fatwa*, passed unanimously (and therefore known as the *muttafiqah fatwa*), that would elicit a government accusation of "conspiracy":

> This meeting of the All-India Khilafat Conference heartily congratulates Ghazi Mustafa Kamal Pasha and the Angora [Ankara] Government upon their magnificent victories and the success of their most desperate (or self-sacrificing) endeavours in upholding the laws of Islam and (this meeting) prays to Almighty God that they may soon succeed in expelling the whole of the armies of the foreign governments from every nook and corner of the Turkish Empire. In addition, this meeting clearly proclaims that it is in every way religiously unlawful for a Mussalman at the present moment to continue in the British Army, or to enter the army, or to induce others to join the army. And it is the duty of (all) Mussalmans in general and the Ulemas in particular to see that these religious commandments are brought home to every Mussalman in the army. Further more, this meeting also announces that if the British Government were to take any military . . . measures against the Angora Government, directly or indirectly, openly or secretly, then the Mussalmans of India will be compelled to commence . . . civil disobedience . . . and to proclaim at the forthcoming annual sessions of the Congress Committee to be held at Ahmedabad the complete independence of India . . . [Akhtar 1971: 105–106].

According to one of the government witnesses present at the meeting, the *fatwa* was supported by some 2000 people: "Mahomedans, Hindus, Pathans, Sikhs, Shikarpuris and Kutchis" (*The Statesman Weekly Edition*, October 21, 1921). The resolution made clear the opposition of the meeting to European actions in the Middle East, the hopes placed by the *'ulama* in the modernizing government of Middle Eastern peoples themselves, and the direct link between their hopes for Turkey and their hopes for their own independence.

In his speech supporting the resolution, Maulana Madani articulated, on the basis of Qur'anic citations, that Muslims were part of a larger Muslim world:

> there is no . . . difference on account of which a Mussalman may remain indifferent . . . to (the fortunes of) the other [Mussalmans] or may leave him in a condition which exposes him or his honour or his property to any danger . . . Mussalmans should stand with one another on the same (friendly) terms as exist between two brothers [Akhtar 1971: 107].

Maulana Madani went on to make clear the divine sanction of refusing to fight Muslims on behalf of those whose intent was to destroy not only Muslim power but Islam – hardly a leap on his part, one might add, given the crusade-like rhetoric of at least some Englishmen (Fromkin 1990: 170). For the novelty of this concept of Muslim solidarity, one need only look at the history of the Indian subcontinent itself, let alone the recent history of Muslims in the armies of their colonial rulers, for many examples to the contrary.

In his speech, Maulana Madani recounted an anecdote told by an Australian Christian who had apparently been in the trenches with two Muslim Indians who quarreled over two or three days until one leapt from his place, threw down his weapons to run to the other side, and, not surprisingly, was shot down by his own side. As in a story of the Sufis, for three nights a candle was seen lit where the "deserter" lay, and, when the body was recovered, it had not decomposed. To refuse to fight Muslims for the Allies, "these enemies of God and the Prophet," was to secure Divine reward (Akhtar 1971: 110–112). And, Maulana Madani added, in an argument that would re-echo in the next world war, India had no reason to be in this war. He had met a Turkish general in Malta who described his shock at the participation of Indian soldiers on the Allied side: "We [i.e. the Turks] had not attacked India. We never in any way injured either the hindus or the mussalmans [sic] of India . . . we were bound up with them by ties of hearts and religion" (Akhtar 1971: 112–113).

Maulana Madani also introduced the theme that would dominate the subsequent trial, namely the rights of Indians to religious freedom:

> The command of Islam is that a Muslim can obey a king who operates within the parameters of Islamic law . . . If we are arrested for serving Islam, then the responsibility will rest with the government and not with us. If the government's desire is to deny religious freedom, then it should openly announce it. In that case, seven crore [70 million] Muslims would have to make their decision either to live as Muslims or as British subjects. Likewise the twenty-two crore Hindus should also decide about their fate. Because when religious freedom is denied, it will be denied to everyone. If Lord Reading [the Viceroy] has been sent [to India] to burn the Qur'an, to efface the *hadith*, and destroy the books of *fiqh*, then I will be the first one to sacrifice [my life] [Rizvi 1980: 100–101].

The seven people most active in supporting the resolution were six Muslims, Maulana Madani, Muhammad 'Ali and his brother Shaukat 'Ali, Dr. Saifuddin Kitchlew, Maulana Nisar Ahmad, and Pir Ghulam Mujaddid; and one Hindu, Sri Shankaracharya. All were charged with conspiracy although they were not immediately arrested. The government's first step was to check dissemination of the resolution, arresting publishers and distributors and confiscating copies.

But arrests followed. By now, the Khilafat organization was sufficiently extensive that volunteers tried, unsuccessfully, to prevent Maulana Madani's arrest when warrants were issued in September (Minault 1982: 164). The arrests gave a great spur to popular action on the grounds of religious freedom. Mahatma Gandhi called for calm. The Jamiat Ulama continued their efforts to assert that the confiscation of the *fatwa* was interference in religion. The dismissive tone of the English-language *Statesman* – "The arrest of the Ali Brothers and others as a week-end thrill was a very bad second to the

Quadrangular Cricket Tournament" – seemed belied by reports in the same paper of protests at Jallianwala Bagh and as far away as Rangoon (*The Statesman Weekly Edition*, September 28, 1921). Restrictions were put in place in Karachi on carrying sticks, collecting stones, singing songs or "haranguing," blocking streets, and approaching or garlanding prisoners.

A hearing was held at the Court of the City Magistrate, Karachi, on September 26, 1921. Since the defendants were "non-cooperators" how could they even participate in the proceedings? To register their position, they chose to offer statements and not engage in the proceedings actively. Dr. Kitchlew chose to speak in Urdu rather than English, intended also as a sign of non-cooperation. Ghulam Mujaddid spoke in Sindhi. The defendants refused to answer questions. The court itself was made a stage for the performance of non-cooperation and for disseminating a wide-ranging critique of government policies.

The statements by the accused argued emphatically the point of the *fatwa* campaign: that the government was interfering unjustly in matters of religion. Muhammad 'Ali's spirited testimony also reviewed what were regarded as breaches of faith on the part of the British government, namely their promise that the Holy Places in the Hijaz would remain free of attack, the retention of the Caliph of specific areas, and, above all, the commitment that Muslim soldiers would not be deployed against Muslim armies in Britain's "crusade."

Maulana Madani's lengthy testimony illustrated that, within roughly a year of his return to India, he had mastered the rhetorical theme of identifying behavior as "religious," a critical category because in colonial India "religion," unlike politics, was in principle an area beyond the control of the colonial state. It would seem from his testimony that, teacher to the end, he basically set out to educate the Magistrate about the Queen's Proclamation of 1858, which was the founding document for the principle of non-interference on the part of the Government of India in the religious lives of her subjects. What he did, Maulana Madani insisted, *was* religion. After the first two minutes, the Magistrate interrupted to say he did not need a lecture, just answers to his questions. But Maulana Madani, who had shifted into scholar's mode, flooded the hapless Magistrate with an onslaught of scriptural quotations and arguments to justify what he was doing on Islamic grounds. The Magistrate periodically interrupted to say, for example, that there was no need to read him the whole Qur'an. Maulana Madani replied firmly that what he was quoting at that point happened to be *hadith* – and on he went. Maulana Madani argued from scripture and used the colonizer's own terms of "tolerance" and "non-interference," a critical theme in the legitimating language of the colonialism of the day.

This was all to no avail. The City Magistrate concluded that there was a prima facie case against all the seven accused "of being parties to a criminal conspiracy to seduce Mohamedan officers and soldiers in the army of His Majesty," along with related charges, and they were therefore committed to the Court of Sessions to stand trial (Akhtar 1971: 104).

The trial in the Sessions Court, which had to be held in an auditorium because of the size of the crowds, began at the end of October. The jurors' names suggest that they were two Hindus, two Christian Indians, and one Englishman. Again, the court was a stage for performing non-cooperation. The defendants refused to plead. They refused to stand when the judge entered. When threatened that their chairs would be removed, they spread their hand-loom *khadi* cloaks on the floor and sat upon them – an act imitated by the onlookers by the second day "when there arose a tottering pyramid of discarded chairs" (*The Statesman Weekly Edition*, November 2, 1921; Minault 1982: 174). This was not to say the defendants were not serious. They were serious about their political position; and they were serious in believing that the court proceeding was a sham. Muhammad 'Ali wept when he asked the jurors, at the conclusion of his speech, to remember that the world was God's and not King George's, and that for the sake of God he would slaughter even "my own dear brother, my dear aged mother, wife, children . . ." (*The Statesman Weekly Edition*, October 5, 1921; Akhtar 1971: 270–271).

Maulana Madani, the second accused, emphasized the importance for him as a scholar to educate others, and to this end he used the courtroom itself to persuade not only the jury but the audience that it was not lawful to serve in the army. True to form, Maulana Madani spoke for over two and a half hours until a recess was called, and then he resumed again (*The Tribune*, November 1, 1921). All, again, to no avail. Sri Shankaracharya, the lone Hindu, was acquitted of all charges. The six others were convicted of abetting the commission of an offence by the public and of making statements conducive to public mischief. They were acquitted on the charge of conspiracy but still sentenced to two years of rigorous imprisonment. English-language newspapers varied in their responses, but *The Independent* (Allahabad) memorably said the detention on "the comparatively flippant and frivolous 'offense' of circulating the statement . . . sounds like comic opera." *The Amrita Bazar Patrika* (Calcutta) saw the whole trial as a blow to the prestige of the Government, and bowed to the accused in "respectful homage" (*The Statesman Weekly Edition*, November 9, 1921). Certainly, the verdict encouraged many followers.

Imprisonment this time was far more difficult in terms of everyday living and interaction than Malta had been. Prisoners were expected to work, and were subjected to severe controls. Maulana Madani, joined by three Hindu "brothers," protested the body searches conducted after prisoners had worked outside. Some accommodation was made but when Maulana Madani continued to object, he was handcuffed during the night and his food reduced to soup. When his protest continued, he was placed in leg irons for a month. It was only after Gandhi wrote in protest in his journal, *Young India*, that the irons were removed. Maulana Madani also undertook a hunger strike to protest the ban on reciting the call to prayer. Several Muslims and, again, a handful of Hindus joined him in the protest. As punishment, he was confined to his cell for six days. In the end, the jailors permitted the prisoners to call *azan* quietly. Maulana Madani's protests had underlined that the jailors were violating prisoners' religious rights (*Maktubat*: I, 105–107).

Released at the end of 1923, Maulana Madani found the euphoria and cooperation that had been sweeping India at the time of his arrest largely dissipated. After some of his followers attacked a police station in the eastern United Provinces town of Chauri Chaura, Gandhi had, to great criticism by some of the *'ulama* and others, called off the non-cooperation campaign on February 12, 1922. Gandhi himself was put in jail. In 1921, there had been violence in the coastal area of Malabar in the southwest, where a combination of economic distress on the part of Muslim peasants and repression by the colonial state produced a violent response interpreted as the work of "fanatic" Mappila Muslim perpetrators. This event ushered in a period of frequent Hindu–Muslim clashes throughout the decade of the 1920s. Aggressive Hindu "reconversion" movements, the *shuddhi* campaigns, were set in motion along with plans to organize Hindus in paramilitary style, *sangathan*. This was met by Muslim *tabligh* ("preaching") and *tanzim* ("organizing") in return. There was also disarray among the political leadership. Some influential figures were ready to turn to violence. Others, especially in Punjab and Bengal, favored participation in the councils set up by the 1919 act. The Khilafat Movement had challenged overall European policy in the Middle East, but its core symbol, the preservation of the *khilafat* in Istanbul, was also about to disappear with the modernizing Turks' own abolition of the caliphate in 1924.

Newly released from jail, Maulana Madani served as president at the fifth annual meeting of the Jamiat Ulama held at Kakinada (in the southeastern coastal region of Andhra), delivering his address on December 29, 1923. He demonstrated that neither the times nor imprisonment had changed his driving conviction. He emphasized the barbarism and exploitation of Europeans, above all the British, in reducing countries like Turkey and Egypt, once prosperous, to poverty. Britain, he argued, had long made Islam and Muslim peoples a particular target. The divisions in India today, above all the Hindu–Muslim division, he laid at Britain's door. He talked of the need for fearless opposition to Britain in the quest for full independence or *swaraj*. To this end he listed two key components: Hindu–Muslim unity on the one hand; *tabligh* and education among

Muslims on the other (Madani 1990: 5–22). Maulana Madani consistently opposed aggressive "re-conversion" and violence, but he contended that dissemination and practice of the great teachings of the historic religious traditions, thwarted in his view by colonialism, was not in conflict with, but intrinsic to, the reclaiming of India's freedom.

CALCUTTA AND SYLHET

At the time of his arrest in 1921, Maulana Madani had been based in Calcutta for roughly a year. His association with Bengal was stimulated by an urgent request from an emissary of Maulana Abul Kalam Azad, who was then chairman of the Calcutta Khilafat Committee. The released prisoners had just arrived in Delhi from Malta. Students of the state-supported Madrasa 'Aliya Calcutta, moved by the fervor of non-cooperation, had apparently boycotted their classes in the hope of establishing a national *madrasa* under the auspices of the Khilafat Committee. They now requested the Shaikhul Hind to secure for them a teacher of *hadith* to serve in this independent school. The Shaikhul Hind apparently approached two or three teachers at the Darul 'Ulum, who demurred, whereupon he asked Maulana Madani to go. Although grieved at the prospect of separation from his beloved elder, now in such poor health, he immediately agreed (Najmu'd-din Islahi 1951: 31).

At the time of parting, the Shaikhul Hind, too weak to rise from his bed, grasped Maulana Madani's hand and pressed it to his head, eyes, and chest and then passed it over his whole body. Immediately, an extraordinary state of consciousness prevailed. "In the judgment of those who know the secrets of the way," the biographer Muhammad Miyan wrote, "this was the special form of bestowing spiritual blessings" (Muhammad Miyan 1999a: 35).

In November 1920, Maulana Madani set out by train for Bengal. His route took him via Amroha, where, at the request of his former teacher, Maulana Khalil Ahmad, he disembarked to find that he was

needed to lend his voice to those trying to cancel a scheduled
Sunni–Shi'a debate. Although Deobandis often participated in anti-
Shi'a debates, Maulana Madani spoke effectively against doing so on
this occasion with the argument that now was a time for solidarity in
the face of British oppression. It was in Amroha, engaged in this effort
at peace making, that Maulana Madani received a telegram from
Dr. Ansari informing him that the Shaikhul Hind had passed away. He
left directly for Deoband, too late to join the funeral prayers. The rector of Deoband, Maulana Hafiz Ahmad, took the opportunity to urge
him to rejoin the staff of the seminary, but Maulana Madani, more
than ever, wanted to fulfill Mahmudul Hasan's final request to him.
He set out again for Calcutta, where he taught the courses on *hadith*
in the new school until his position was terminated because of his
trial and imprisonment (*Naqsh-i hayat*: II, 261–273).

After his release from prison in 1924, Maulana Madani returned
to eastern India. In a letter in 1924 to a fellow Islamic scholar,
Maulana Madani wrote that a group of graduates of the Madrasa
'Aliya, well-trained in modern subjects and Arabic, some familiar
with English, like the earlier group he had responded to in Calcutta,
had implored him to come to Sylhet, a Muslim area on the Assam
border. The inhabitants, they explained, were hard-working, like
Hindu Bengalis, but needed someone to teach them *hadith*. Rather
than the easier course of working in one of the established Deobandi
madrasas, Maulana Madani, now remarried, agreed to settle in Sylhet
along with his wife. As time allowed, he spoke publicly and attended
meetings, but organizational work now receded in favor of education, somewhat like Gandhi's retreat from public life during the
upheavals of the mid-1920s.

Maulana Madani worried about this choice. He had, to be sure,
first resorted to *istikhara*, opening the Qur'an at random for an
omen. But he was troubled by a dream that a friend had had and
reported to him. The dreamer had seen himself, the Shaikhul Hind,
and Maulana Madani sitting together on a platform. The Shaikhul
Hind said to Maulana Madani that he had a separate prayer rug, and
indeed there it was on one side. The Shaikhul Hind and the man

recounting the dream then picked up a prayer rug, went inside the house, and spread it out on a platform there. Nearby was a sleeping child, whom the Shaikhul Hind covered with a large quilt. Hearing this, Maulana Madani felt that he had to ask himself if it could be the case that the Shaikhul Hind was not pleased with his focus on educational work and had taken his protective shadow from him (*Naqsh-i hayat*: II, 245–249). Maulana Madani had in fact taken up a public role different from either the putative *jihad* on the frontier or the Congress–Khilafat–Jamiat Ulama engagement with national politics. His focus now was on the internal strengthening – moral, material, and physical – of the Muslim population.

Maulana Madani held fast to his decision, not only to teach at a *madrasa* but to try to reach Muslims beyond the *madrasa* with a message of organization and reform. In Bengal he would set out through the difficult terrain of fields, rivers, and creeks, particularly dangerous during the rains, to preach and teach. He would, according to one biographer, arrive in a village and even if only a handful of people turned out, he would "preach on the *sunnat* with the joy and enthusiasm as if it were thousands." He was given credit for influencing some two dozen *madrasas* in Sylhet to offer a high level of Arabic instruction and to require Qur'anic recitation. He also used his influence to see that the students drilled in "parade" as volunteers and, using sticks, learned the martial art of "*binaut*" (Najmu'd-din Islahi 1951: 49). This was typical of the physical culture and discipline that appeared within India and worldwide in the interwar years.

In a 1926 letter, written from the Khilafat office in Sylhet to his former teacher, Maulana Khalil Ahmad, Maulana Madani spelled out his vision for disseminating correct practices among Muslims and for fortifying them for self-defense as necessary. He emphasized Muslim weakness, and denied Hindu claims, given their overwhelming numbers and economic superiority, that they were threatened. Muslims had to follow their example of organizing. For this organizing (*tanzim*), he suggested that every urban quarter or every sub-group (*qaum*), as appropriate, make participation in the canonical prayer and maintenance of mosques their focus. There should be three or four individuals who would take the main responsibility. In addition each of these units should make a census showing the number of Muslim households, noting which were observant, which were literate, and which employed, as a resource for pursuing their goals.

Second, he recommended the organization of a body of "volunteers" (the English word was used) to be trained in service and protection. They too should learn martial skills and take an oath to render service to Islam and Muslims. Again the nucleus should be the neighborhood or *qaum*, now headed by an elected *jam'adar* to whom others pledged their obedience. The unit should help anywhere in the city as needed, take part in national processions or meetings, and attempt to resolve peacefully any disputes that might emerge. They should provide protection if attacked. There should be a "captain" of all the *jam'adars* in a city who would be under the direction of the head of the Khilafat Committee (since the Khilafat infrastructure persisted for several years after the abolition of the caliphate) (Hasan and Pernau 2005).

Third, he provided rules for an organization for "reform of expenditure." He was concerned with the indebtedness of Muslims, using as his example the peasants of the Punjab. Among the many harmful aspects of this, he argued, was the inability of Muslims to marry and hence the failure to renew the Muslim population; he provided comparative figures on Muslim and Hindu marriage to prove his point. He particularly targeted the wasteful expenditures of the marriage celebration and spelled out in detail appropriate practices, including the kinds of refreshments that should be offered; the need to do without elephants, litters, and horses; the inappropriateness of fireworks, music, and dancing, and so forth. He specified for whom outfits should be provided, the suitable amount of jewelry and of dowry, restrictions on customary prestations to servants and family, and the need to eliminate the events typically celebrated in the wedding's aftermath. As Deobandis had done for decades, he urged that the new couple be set up in property or trade with the money that otherwise would have been wasted. Earlier reformers had stressed moral reasons for not engaging in excess expenditures, particularly the importance of not acting out of pride and the desire for display (Thanawi 1992: 112–144). Maulana Madani, in contrast, emphasized the problem of economic ruin. He continued with guidance on expenditures for other occasions of life-cycle ceremonies and worship. There should be a managing committee to work out these matters for each city or *qaum*.

Maulana Madani believed that Muslims – "poor, unemployed, ignorant, oblivious, few in numbers" – were dangerously weak and that other communities would like to see "the voice of Muslims gone from the country of India." For him, those who were ready, as he put it, to conduct a funeral procession for Hindu–Muslim unity had forgotten that their real enemy was the British, and that Muslims themselves needed to awake if they wanted to avoid a very dark future. He urged his fellow Muslims to organize in order to check "their ignorance, disunity, wastefulness, and absorption in court cases." Muslims at this point, he argued, should do business only with other Muslims in order to overcome their economic backwardness. He would devote himself full-time to such organizing, he explained, were he not employed, and his purpose in writing to his old teacher and influential friend was to urge him and his associates to action since the point of learning was not only, as he put it, one's own reform but that of others as well (*Maktubat*: IV, 283–294).

Although the alliterative pairs, *shuddhi* and *sangathan* and *tanzim* and *tabligh*, are often treated as equivalent, Muslims did, indeed, start from a weaker point both in terms of numbers and economic position. They were also weaker, one might argue, because of the important strand in cultural nationalism that pictured Hindus as the only "real" citizens of India. In the colonial period, Muslims were increasingly conflated with the British as "foreigners." In any case, in terms of organizing there was nothing like a Muslim equivalent to the aggressive *shuddhi* to convert outsiders on the part of the Arya Samaj or other Hindu groups, nor did any of the Muslim efforts at military-style organization, however much Maulana Madani may have wished it, take root as did, for example, the Hindu nationalist organizing in the Rashtriya Sevak Sangh, which persists to the present. There were,

however, many organizations that undertook *tabligh* to other
Muslims, an effort that seems to have had little influence in these
decades but that would emerge as a significant strategy of Muslim
Indians after Independence.

PRINCIPAL OF DEOBAND

In 1927 the *madrasa* at Deoband faced a crisis of leadership. Maulana
Anwar Shah Kashmiri (1875–1933), the principal, was one of the
pre-eminent Islamic scholars of twentieth-century India, a prolific
writer, and a gifted teacher. Like Maulana Madani, he was a graduate
of the school, a disciple of Rashid Ahmad Gangohi, and in 1909 had,
like him, returned to the school at the urgent request of the leadership. He had stayed at Deoband in the intervening years, and now he
was caught up in a bitter controversy related to a student strike. In
the end, Maulana Hafiz Mohammad Ahmad and Maulana Habibur
Rahman, the key administrators, decided to bring in a new principal,
and they turned to Maulana Madani.

At this point, Anwar Shah left Deoband along with several other faculty members, including Maulana Shabbir Ahmad 'Usmani
(1885–1949), and departed to Dhabeel, in Gujarat, where they would
establish what would prove to be a successful and long-lived Darul
'Ulum. Anwar Shah continued to share the political commitments
of the other Deobandi *'ulama*. During these years of great political
uncertainty, he delivered the presidential address to the Peshawar
meeting of the Jamiat Ulama in 1927, confirming the Jamiat's
unwavering theme of the importance of Hindu–Muslim unity and
analyzing at length the Prophet's alliance with the Jews of Medina in
the document known as the Constitution of Medina as a relevant model
for the times (Anwar Shah 2004). After only five years in Dhabeel, he
became ill and returned to Deoband, where he passed away in 1933.

Having seen that differences could emerge at the school, and having
come to some clarity as to what his own priorities were, Maulana
Madani set out some twenty-nine terms before he agreed to return to

the school. To the extent that there were some at the school still determined to stay apart from any political activity, Maulana Madani made
clear that he would act otherwise. He would not, he said, spend more
than two to three hours a day on the work of the *madrasa*; he would regularly spend one week a month as well as the annual vacation on the
national movement; and he would have nothing whatsoever to do with
the colonial government. There would be no requirement that he
resign from any organization. He wanted no obstacle placed in his way
to organizing the students for practice in debate, speeches, essay writing, and studying current events. He made it clear that he might not
attend meetings, nor would he be responsible for routine administration, although he expected his opinions to be honored. He would not
engage in fund-raising. He should be provided with any books or other
materials necessary for his scholarship. Any time he failed to meet his
classes should be deducted from his salary. He gave the school a week
to reply, and they responded with the astute answer that he should simply serve the school as had the Shaikhul Hind (Madani 1967 [?]: 3–7).

MASS POLITICS, MINORITY POLITICS

Maulana Madani had returned to India at a point of dramatic political
change. The turn toward mass participation in political life, in which
Gandhi's role was central, had been launched. Transnational engagements of many kinds increasingly shaped what was happening in
India. Maulana Madani and other Muslim political figures now saw
themselves increasingly as part of a worldwide Muslim population.
As a minority, the Muslims of India were not alone in this interwar
era in looking to some larger international world to enhance their
status within their own nation. In a different national context,
African Americans, for example, in a range of Africa-focused movements, did much the same, as did other beleaguered groups, like
women and workers, whose international organizations took on new
importance in the interwar years as a way of gaining leverage in their
specific countries.

The British Empire, however, was of decreasing importance as a transnational space that Indian nationalists embraced. Gandhi in South Africa, for example, had long attempted to establish Indian rights in terms of a status owed them as imperial subjects. Now, instead, Maulana Madani and others emphasized the empire as a place of systemic exploitation. In part based on his own sojourns before and after Malta, Husain Ahmad wrote that the British in Egypt had simultaneously turned ethno-religious groups against each other and reduced the whole population to helplessness "like bangle-wearing women, just like the population of India." He went on to say that the British, in contrast to exploitative kings of old, had secured an unprecedented depth of control in every dimension of life. Yet they posed, he said, as "goddesses of justice," whose angels sing a "raga" of the history of "progress and humanity" (*Asir-i Malta*: 99–102).

As noted above, Britain in the course of the Great War had seemed to support the transnational expectation that "self-determination" was appropriate to its colonies. Britain in fact drew back significantly from this, as evident in the modest gains offered in the Montagu–Chelmsford Reforms of 1919. One of the most significant interventions in attempting to show India "unfit" for self-rule, now known to have had official support, was the 1927 publication presuming to expose India's innate depravity, the American Katherine Mayo's blockbuster, *Mother India* (Sinha 2006). India's troubles, this sensationalist work argued, were the fruit of Hinduism, against which, implicitly, colonialism was the only check. A central response to this was an Indian campaign to confront one of Mayo's charges by legislating the criminalization of child marriage. This campaign demonstrated that it was not Indians, but the colonial regime claiming non-interference in religion, that was the obstacle to social advance. Maulana Madani and others of the Jamiat Ulama-i-Hind, however, held aloof from this campaign, arguing that the issue was irrelevant to Muslims since among Muslims the girl's consent was in principle required for a marriage. While an understandable effort to defend inherent Islamic teachings, such a stance isolated Muslims from what was essentially a nationalist campaign.

The decade as a whole saw sustained social unrest, including Hindu–Muslim disturbances, which, like the Mapilla riots that inaugurated the decade, in some cases had an economic base and were as much fueled as contained by colonial interventions. In addition, there were substantial peasant movements as well as industrial unrest, with protesters more focused on their serious grievances than on the nationalist movement. Communist and trades union protest in particular met with severe repression. These were issues that neither the Congress leadership nor the 'ulama made central in their campaigns. Their attention was riveted at the end of the decade by the prospect of further constitutional change. The process was ushered in by the shocking appointment in 1927, the same year as the publication of *Mother India*, of the commission to recommend further constitutional change. The "Simon Commission" included not a single Indian representative.

In response, Indian nationalists sought to make their own proposals, most notably in the "Nehru Report," named for its author, Motilal Nehru (father of the nationalist leader and future prime minister, Jawaharlal). It differed from the demands of the Jamiat Ulama in two significant ways, first in its goal of dominion status, not complete independence, and second by its proposal to end *both* separate electorates and reservation of seats as well as its preference for a strong center (which would check some degree of Muslim autonomy in Muslim-majority provinces). Maulana Madani was among those who criticized the Report. For the so-called nationalist 'ulama (and, in fact, at this point the Muslim League), the end of separate electorates was appropriate, but reservations for minorities in elected bodies at least for a time seemed essential. For the 'ulama, moreover, only complete independence was acceptable, a position the Congress would also adopt in the following year.

Maulana Madani in the first decade after his return from Malta had undertaken a life unlike anything that had gone before in his active role in grassroots teaching, on the one hand, and in national political organizations on the other. He now was seen, and saw himself, as an "Indian Muslim," an identity intensified by the very issues, like the *khilafat*, social reform, and constitutional arrangements, that defined the decade. Like other nationalists, he proved his credibility by defiance of colonial authorities and imprisonment. Like Gandhi, he also devoted himself to grassroots "constructive" work of education and moral reform, in his case primarily in Sylhet. His was an explicit shoring up of an Islamic identity, which he saw as not only morally imperative but foundational for the future state. At the same time he kept up his *madrasa*-based activities, honed during his years in Medina and, at the end of the decade, based again in Deoband.

As a core administrator and teacher at the most important *madrasa* in India, he was committed, as he saw it, to the production of the only class of leaders who could authentically guide their fellow Muslims in their moral and spiritual lives. As president of the Jamiat Ulama-i-Hind and principal of the *madrasa* at Deoband, Maulana Madani was increasingly referred to as the "Shaikhul Islam," a title that recalled Maulana Mahmudul Hasan as "Shaikhul Hind," but that identified him specifically with "Islam." This title, typically in a Muslim polity given to the official responsible for overseeing *qazis*, pious endowments, and so forth, pointed to the kind of cultural autonomy the *'ulama* envisaged for each religious community in the future state.

WHO SPEAKS FOR MUSLIMS?
THE CHALLENGES OF
THE 1930s

The decade of the thirties was marked by deliberations on all sides over the political future of India. Muslim leaders for the most part opposed British rule, although a range of emerging movements simultaneously challenged the increasing dominance of the Congress party. Muslim leaders competed for the support of other Muslims, not Indians generally, as the structure of colonized society, including the system of separate Muslim electorates, virtually required them to do. Their debates with each other were not only about political strategies and ideals. They were also about the credibility of people who claimed to speak for Muslims and Islam.

From the perspective of someone like Maulana Madani, many of those now claiming to speak for Islam lacked authority. Among them were figures like the westernized lawyer Muhammad Ali Jinnah (1876–1948), leader of the Muslim League, and the poet Iqbal (1877–1938), as well as new figures on the stage in the 1930s like the "Islamist" Abul A'la Maududi (1903–1979) and the leader of the militant Khaksar, 'Inayatullah Mashriqi (1888–1963). In every case these figures had scant respect for the *ulama*. From Madani's perspective, for them to seek political leadership was one thing; arrogating to themselves the role of interpreting Islam was something else. They, however, dismissed someone like Maulana Madani and others of the 'ulama because of their alleged lack of the worldly experience and the "modernity" that they themselves claimed.

When these leaders made Islamic arguments, it was in the "modernist" style that ignored the traditionalist scholarly heritage in favor of direct interpretation of sacred texts. Maulana Madani's writings in these years make clear that an increasing part of his concern was an insistence that Islamic leadership properly belonged to one professional category, the 'ulama, not another, namely that of the secularly educated.

In this decade there were not only challenges to the authority of the 'ulama, there also began to be serious political divergences among the traditionalist 'ulama themselves. By the end of the decade, even Deobandi scholars ceased to speak with a unified voice as some among them opted to support the Muslim League and what had begun to emerge as the idea of dividing India. Since the political differences that were now emerging among the 'ulama themselves could not be attributed to the differences of discourse and education that marked off the western-educated, at times their conflicts resolved into ones over personal characteristics. From this perspective, for his followers, Maulana Madani's very person powerfully communicated prophetic revelation, bringing to life Islamic symbols and memories among his followers.

MAULANA MADANI'S CHARACTER

There is no way to understand Maulana Madani's influence in these years apart from his intellectual and spiritual role. At Deoband he now served as both principal and the head teacher of hadith, the position that Maulana Mahmudul Hasan had once held. The teaching of hadith was the very heart of the academic experience at Deoband. As the source of prophetic models and injunctions, it was nothing less than the guide to the reformist project that had animated the Deobandis from the start. Despite his political commitments, Maulana Madani continued his pattern of tireless teaching. Those who knew him recalled how, if he had traveled, as he so often did, even if the journey was as far as Sylhet, even if he arrived in the blazing heat of summer, he would resume a class immediately upon arrival. Even on an ordinary day, students would come early to the class, watching the gate for his arrival as he would approach fresh from the congregational prayer, accompanied by students and others eager to hear his conversation (Goyal 2004: 136–140). If he were returning from a trip, one student wrote, the entire school would be abuzz when the word came that he was about to arrive: "For us this was nothing less than '*Id*, our eyes blessed with coolness from seeing this moon of knowledge and piety, the teacher of 'Arab and 'Ajam, the glorious *hadith* scholar, the Junaid of the times . . ." (Muhammad Zahidul Hasani 2003: 156).

Jinn, the created beings invisible to the eye who, like humans, comprise the good and the bad, apparently attended his classes, a theory put out by those who observed him occasionally uttering a word in a direction that suggested their presence. These particular long-lived *jinn* were understood to date from the time of the founder of the Hanafi tradition in the eighth century ('Azizu'r-Rahman 1958: 100–102). The presence of such extraordinary figures would have been an indication of Maulana Madani's fidelity to Hanafi interpretations and practices, a confirmation to his followers of the legitimacy both of his Deobandi orientation and of his particular role as teacher and guide.

Jinn aside, Maulana Madani was known in these years as someone who maintained a vast and growing web of relationships. One biographer later organized vignettes of these relationships by categories, sorting out his relationships with the poor, servants, children, friends, officials, fellow prisoners, fellow travelers, colleagues in the Jamiat and at Deoband, and, indeed, *jinn* ('Azizu'r-Rahman 1958: 72–101). The stories range from the simple acts of everyday life to events that anyone would gloss as miracles, all designed to show Maulana Madani's holiness and embodiment of *shari'a*. For example, on one occasion Maulana Madani was in the midst of a meeting with his associates when a little daughter, learning to walk, stumbled

while coming into the room. He stopped what he was doing to lov-
ingly pick her up. A simple story like this one took on transcendent
meaning to a disciple who recalled the Prophet Muhammad's inter-
rupting a sermon to comfort his grandson who had similarly tripped
('Azizu'r-Rahman 1958: 81).

The train, one might note, was crucial to sustaining Maulana
Madani's many ties: he traveled to the original family home in Tanda;
to Sylhet, where he tried to spend the holy month of Ramadan; and
to the meetings of the Jamiat Ulama-i-Hind, the Congress, Muslim
voluntary associations, meetings at other *madrasas*, and various political gatherings throughout India. No wonder that after a Congress
ministry was set up in 1937, Maulana Madani directed the attention
of the new provincial minister for communications to the need for a
good road from the railway station to the *madrasa* on the occasion of
his visit to Deoband (Rizvi 1980: 226–227).

Equally crucial to his relationships was the post. In 1951 newspaper notices and word-of-mouth requested people who had kept
Maulana Madani's letters to make them available for copying and for
publication. Four dense volumes of letters were published in a single
collection, and one can easily imagine that they represent only a
modest percentage of those that were written over his lifetime, day
after day. For the most part, we see only his side of the correspondence, but from that we build a picture of his relationships to far-
flung followers, a handful from as far as Arabia or South Africa, but
most across the north from the Frontier to Assam. Over years, sometimes decades, his followers depended on him for advice on their
religious obligations, their reading, their relationships to parents and
children and wives, as well as on legal issues of inheritance, dowry,
and property. One series of letters to a single correspondent begins
with a letter to a correspondent so despondent that he is contem-
plating suicide and continues over the years with deeply sympathetic
advice on prayers, self-control, fortitude in suffering, customary
ceremonies, and choosing a bride. Many of the letter writers
sought guidance on spiritual practices and disciplines, legal matters,
and the competing political ideologies of the day. There are letters of

condolence, of concern for family crises, and of sympathy that particularly carry a humane tone that recipients would have cherished. The recipients kept these letters not only for their content, but also as charisma-filled talismans of a holy person.

But views of Maulana Madani like these were not uncontested. Attacks on him came from those who favored an apolitical role for the *'ulama* as well as those who specifically opposed his support for Congress. These opponents not only criticized his politics, as such, but also put out claims that he was irresponsible toward his duties at Deoband, hypocritical in his self-presentation, and even dishonest. Against these critics, Maulana Madani persevered in favoring an active role for the *'ulama* in simultaneously fostering Islamic education and Muslim support for Congress.

NON-COOPERATION AND ROUND TABLES

The decade began with the decision of the Congress to work toward complete independence, officially promulgated on January 26, 1930, accompanied by a second campaign of non-cooperation. The movement won widespread participation, including involvement for the first time of large numbers of women. The Great Depression, which fell hard on agriculturalists and small businessmen, provided an incentive to those impacted to resist taxation and other forms of cooperation. This new campaign was inaugurated in March by Gandhi's dramatic march to the sea to distill salt water in defiance of the heavy duty levied on this everyday necessity. The procession was covered sympathetically by the international media, and acts of similar disobedience spread across the country. Arrests, starting with Gandhi, were swift and many.

Muslim participation in the campaign was limited. Not only did Muslim League leaders stand apart, as they did during the first campaign, but others now withheld support on the grounds that agreement on constitutional arrangements for minorities in free India had to come first. Of these dissenters, Maulana Muhammad 'Ali,

Maulana Madani's colleague in the Khilafat Movement and Karachi trial, was particularly influential, to the point that supporters nominated him for the presidency of the Jamiat Ulama in 1930. This move was strongly opposed by Maulana Madani and others on the formal ground that Muhammad 'Ali, who had not had *madrasa* training, was not one of the *'ulama*. He was, to be sure, addressed as "Maulana," but this was only a courtesy title accorded him when he abandoned the western dress of an England-returned, Aligarh graduate and espoused the Islamic cause of the *khilafat*. In the end, the annual meeting, held in Amroha in May 1930, faced dissension at the meeting itself as well as defection of a splinter group of dissidents who made Muhammad 'Ali their president at a separate meeting. The core meeting resolved fully to join hands with the Congress. Maulana Madani and others argued that this decision was not only pragmatic, if Muslims wanted to be a part of the new nation, but also morally incumbent on them in light of the Prophet's example of cooperation with non-Muslims in a shared polity. Maulana Madani subsequently traveled the country widely to encourage support for this stance in the face of substantial attacks that he and his colleagues were no more than "slaves of the Hindus" (Rashid Hasan 1957: 155).

In addition to the Jamiat Ulama, two other major Muslim organizations allied themselves with the Congress as active participants in non-cooperation. One was the Majlis-i Ahrar, closely tied to the Deobandis and especially significant in the Punjab. Formed in 1929, the Ahrar not only stressed Indian freedom but also the need to address the interests of the poor. In the early 1930s, they took up the plight of Muslims in Kashmir, whose interests were deliberately suppressed by the Hindu maharaja, as they made forays into the princely state and courted arrest. They also targeted the influential Ahmadi sect who were regarded not only as theologically suspect but as loyalists to a repressive regime. Maulana Ata'ullah Shah Bukhari (1892–1961), the Ahrar leader, was acclaimed as a particularly brilliant orator.

The second pro-Congress party was the extraordinary Khuda'i Khidmatgar among the Pathans of the Frontier. Its leader, Khan

Abdul Ghaffar Khan (1890–1988), began his career with a focus on educational reform, but with the post-war repression and the beginnings of non-cooperation, he embraced the Congress political agenda and specifically the program of Gandhian non-cooperation. The Pathans faced brutally harsh repression at the hands of the British in 1930, which they met with an unflinching non-violent response. Given the stereotypical understanding of the Pathans as violent fighters, this level of discipline won widespread popular admiration.

In March 1931, Gandhi agreed to a "pact" between himself and the viceroy, Lord Irwin, promising to suspend non-cooperation and to attend a "Round Table Conference" in London on the future of constitutional reforms. The Jamiat Ulama in August 1931, in anticipation of this imminent meeting, spelled out its own fourteen-point formula for the future state, the basis of its position throughout the years that followed. At the heart of their plan was the goal of making religious education, endowments, and places of worship the purview of the various religious communities. Separate religiously defined personal law was to be preserved, with *qazis* appointed to adjudicate Muslim issues. A Supreme Court would arbitrate issues related to minority rights. They supported universal suffrage. On the vexed question of reservations, the Jamiat opposed the reduction of the Muslim proportion of seats in Bengal and Punjab below their majority. They favored no reservation in those provinces, and reservation by population proportion elsewhere where Muslims were a minority but had previously received "weightage" in their favor (as Hindus had had in Punjab and Bengal). They favored regularizing the status of the NWFP, Baluchistan, and Sind as provinces (which would thus, with Bengal and Punjab, constitute five Muslim-majority entities). Residuary powers should be granted to the provinces. Separate electorates should be ended.

The Round Table accomplished little. The position of the *'ulama* was not represented, nor was Congress able to secure Muslims among their delegates. Gandhi had fought hard to include among the delegates Dr. M. A. Ansari, the western-educated physician who was closely tied to the Deobandis and a member of the

Jamiat Ulama-i-Hind. Despite the fact that Ansari was at that point President of the Congress, Gandhi had no success. The British would increasingly marginalize "Congress Muslims" as independence approached. Nonetheless, the London meeting did give Congress the status of legitimate representative of an emerging nation, a development not everyone welcomed. A new viceroy, the rigid conservative, Lord Willingdon, was determined to show that Britain was still in command. By 1932 Gandhi was again in jail, national organizations including the Jamiat Ulama were proscribed, and repression was widespread. Some 40,000 Indians were arrested within three months.

One strategy of the non-cooperation movement at this point entailed the deliberate courting of arrest on the part of individual leaders of nationalist organizations. During this campaign, apparently, the government tried to avoid arrests of Muslims, especially high-profile ones, in order to spread the impression that Muslims were not in support of Congress non-cooperation (Muhammad Miyan 2005: 149). This made it the more important to play out arrests for visibility and for opportunities to mock official authority.

Maulana Madani made public that he was going to Delhi to the Jami' Masjid to preach in support of non-cooperation, hoping to attract official attention in a very public setting. The police opted to arrest him en route, avoiding the station in Deoband because of the crowds of admirers seeing him off. At the first stop, however, Maulana Madani was handed an official "notice," which he rejected on the grounds that he had to have a translation. The police officer asked to borrow Madani's pen to write it out, but he joked that he was unwilling to supply the weapon for his own execution, a *bon mot* readily repeated. Served then with the translation further down the line at Muzaffarnagar, Maulana Madani this time pointed out that the notice was issued in a different district and thus no longer valid. A new notice was provided in time to finally arrest him.

Something of the dedication of Madani's followers comes through in the account of the subsequent courting of arrest of his disciple, Rashid Hasan 'Usmani. Rashid Hasan first went to Delhi, hoping to be part of the crowd at the Jami' Masjid, only to be thwarted by Maulana Madani's arrest en route. Chagrined at having not traveled with his *shaikh*, Rashid Hasan retreated to the Jamiat office where he found that the leaders had gotten a copy of Maulana Madani's proposed talk, prudently written out in advance. Thereupon, they entrusted him with delivering it. He managed to do so, and afterward somehow slipped past the policemen surrounding the mosque as he left. An officer soon arrived at the Jamiat office, serving Rashid Hasan with a "notice" that he was to leave Delhi within twelve hours or face arrest. Eager as he was to stay, the others insisted he leave. Back in Deoband, he was served with a "notice" again, this time directing him to absent himself from Deoband for a month. He chose Muzaffarnagar, the town where his *shaikh* was imprisoned.

When Maulana Madani was let out after about two weeks, he directed Rashid Hasan to speak publicly. At last he too was arrested – to Maulana Madani's amusement at the comedy of his having wandered around escaping the government's clutches and then finally getting trapped. "Allah, Allah," Rashid Hasan wrote, "this is the special servant of the Lord who considers jail no more than a joke" (Rashid Hasan 1957: 157).

IZHAR-I HAQIQAT, "A DECLARATION OF TRUTH"

The campaign to discredit Maulana Madani developed considerable momentum by the mid-1930s. Rumors, fueled by the Urdu press, were apparently circulating in Burma, the Deccan, and Punjab, as well as in Delhi and areas closer to home. Complaints were sent to political leaders and to the Darul 'Ulum's governing council. Finally, in October and November 1935, Maulana Madani published in the official newspaper of the Jamiat Ulama-i-Hind, *Al Jamiat*, several installments replying to the "propaganda" (he used the English term) against him. These were then re-published as "A Declaration of Truth" in a pamphlet of about fifty pages. Something of Maulana Madani's voice, his driving conviction of the value of both his scholarly and political role, and his zest for meeting an attack head-on emerges in the text (Madani 2004a).

One Hajji Daud Hashim Yusuf of Rangoon was a central figure in drafting the critique, mocking Maulana Madani by calling him by the self-deprecating signature that Maulana Madani himself used, "the Disgrace of the Predecessors" (*nang-i aslaf*), prefaced in this case by "the revered" (*hazrat*). Maulana Madani replied in kind, speaking of himself in the third person as "*nang-i aslaf*" and pointing out more than once that when the Hajji invited him to Rangoon it was with the condition that Maulana Madani say nothing against the government. He similarly noted the interest of a newspaper like the daily *Inqilab* of Lahore in sensationalizing a story to sell newspapers and to placate their anti-Congress supporters.

The detailed attacks accused Maulana Madani of teaching only twelve or fifteen days a month, or even less, and being paid full-time. He taught, the Hajji wrote, all of Bukhari Sharif (one of the primary texts of *hadith*) in only twenty-five days, yet – "a miracle" – all students passed, until a newspaper pointed this out and grades were secretly changed. His thousands of disciples and former students (*murid, shagird*) gave him money, which he failed to transmit to the Darul 'Ulum. Instead, dressed in *khadi* and a "Gandhi cap," thus feigning austerity, he distributed this wealth as if it was from his own income.

In April 1935, the Hajji posed his queries and complaints about Maulana Madani to Maulana Shabbir Ahmad 'Usmani, the patron of the Darul 'Ulum, asking for details about governance and, specifically, where a teacher got the right to make religious students follow his wrong path (*maslak*) of Congress and Gandhi, an influence he estimated extended to 70 percent of the students. The coffers of Deoband were now empty, he concluded, because of the widespread conviction that all of Deoband followed the Congress *maslak*. A further complaint asked for comment on newspaper reports that *madrasa* students were stealing fans and seats from trains and taking them back to their lodgings. The school's administration replied by sending the Hajji information on the terms agreed on when Maulana Madani was hired.

Maulana Madani's own defense showed him as someone who thought of himself as part of a professional class. He had negotiated terms, he pointed out, at a time when he had eight or nine other job offers. Why shouldn't a teacher have the right to negotiate his job the way any other worker does? If there were objections to the terms, he noted, that was a matter for the managers who had accepted them, not for him. He also suggested a comparison of his teaching schedule with the schedules of teachers and professors at western-style schools and universities.

In relation to his teaching, Maulana Madani drew on the "registers" and records, which implicitly demonstrated the careful bureaucratic management of the Darul 'Ulum. He provided a chart of annual enrollments and pointed out that in the past twenty years the number of *hadith* students at Deoband had more than tripled. The increased number of students made for more exams to grade. Since among them were advanced students who came to Deoband after attending other *madrasas*, he taught longer hours. If he was so flawed, he asked, why do students leave their homes and come here when there are so many other good teachers and so many other *madrasas*? He also provided details about comparable schools where two teachers typically covered the materials he alone taught. He dismissed as nonsense the reports on the number of sessions devoted to Bukhari, the success rate of students (failures were in the typical range of frequency), and any suggestion of doctoring the register. He also pointed out some eight categories of administrative committees and other obligations at the school that the critics seemed unaware of that also impacted his teaching hours.

Maulana Madani provided a precise record of his activities month by month for the entire preceding year, a window into the political meetings, electioneering, and organizations that he was active in; he also noted the number of trips that he was able to complete during the weekly and annual holidays. He insisted that many of his absences were in relation to religious activities that were counted as part of the work of his predecessors, like meetings at other *madrasas*. Meetings of organizations like the Jamiat Ulama-i-Hind, he maintained, rightly should also be counted as part of the duties of someone like himself now. He noted days of missed teaching when, as happened twice during the year, a student died. He also undertook two fact-finding trips to garner correct information should there be need to make official appeals: one, for a week, following the catastrophic Bihar earthquake (which hit on January 15, 1934) and one to the contested site of Babar's mosque in Ayodhya. He challenged his opponents to name other university professors or *madrasa* teachers who kept up this level of activity of religious service.

As for funds, he documented the amount of money he had received as explicit donations to the school and transmitted accordingly. He also pointed out that he did indeed keep and allocate funds from donors who specifically told him that they wanted him to find worthy recipients in need. He did not, he said, consider "*khadr poshi*" and "*Gandhi kep*" a matter deserving taunts.

At the end of the pamphlet, Maulana Madani answered complaints about governance at the school and about his own political influence. Although he did not name him in the pamphlet, the leading Islamic scholar opposing Muslim support for Congress was Maulana Ashraf 'Ali Thanawi (1863–1943). Maulana Thanawi was one of the most influential Deobandis of the century, a prolific writer and the spiritual and moral guide for innumerable followers. In these years, he was serving as the school's patron. Maulana Madani never deviated in his respect for him, and, indeed, in reproducing his schedule for the previous year, he noted that he had traveled to Thana Bhawan to consult with Maulana Thanawi about the latter's pamphlet, *Al Hilatun Najiza*. This was a document of great importance in providing alternatives to apostasy for wives seeking divorce, one of the landmark documents demonstrating judicial responsiveness to changing circumstances on the part of the Deobandi *'ulama* and a prelude to a significant legislative act on Muslim divorce (Zaman 2002: 29–31, 205–208). Maulana Thanawi was deeply skeptical of the plunge of his fellow *'ulama* into politics, and specifically distrusted cooperation with Hindus, who, he believed, would always keep Muslims subordinate in the Indian context.

In 1935, new guidelines were issued by the administration of the Darul 'Ulum that reduced the authority of the patron in favor of that of the council. Maulana Thanawi by the end of the year had resigned. Maulana Madani justified the new guidelines as a reassertion of the democratic order (*jamhuri nizam*) intended by the founders. His very language is a clue of the extent to which he was part of the emerging political culture of the times.

Yet committed as he was to concepts like democracy, he never wavered in his conviction that political behavior for Muslims had to be shaped by Islamic values. The colonial government had legislated a prohibition on the use of undue religious influence in political campaigning, but Madani had no hesitation in defending his political influence on the students precisely as a religious obligation, specifically the obligation incumbent on an Islamic scholar to teach what he believes to be morally right. He used technical legal terms in defense of his influence: "If in a scholar's opinion wearing a Gandhi cap is preferable (*mustahabb*) or proper (*wajib*) or obligatory (*farz*), it is his absolute obligation to exert himself so that not even one student in a hundred [not the thirty that the Hajji had complained about] remains" (Madani 2004a: 600). As for donations to the school being down, according to Maulana Madani, the Hajji had the reason backward: it was because ordinary Muslims had come to believe that the people at the school were slaves of the British.

THE ELECTIONS OF 1936

After the problematic results of their consultations in the early 1930s, the British moved forward to restructure the government on their own with a plan to retain control at the Center while awarding Indians full control in the provinces. In 1935 they issued a new Government of India Act. The proposed Center outlined in the Act in fact never came into effect, primarily because of princely and

Muslim fears, but elections for provincial legislatures, with an elec-
torate considerably increased to some thirty million voters, took
place in 1937. The system of separate electorates for Muslims, much
condemned by both the Congress and the Jamiat, was continued.

Jinnah, who had just returned to India after five years in England,
faced the problem that the Muslim League had virtually no popular
base. Despite deep reservations about the aristocratic bent and loyal-
ism of the League, Congress and other Muslim parties forged a deal
to cooperate with it on the assumption that they shared fundamental
nationalist goals. The Jamiat leadership, including Maulana Madani,
agreed to support the League candidates upon assurances from
Jinnah himself that the League would defer to the Jamiat on matters
related to religion and would reshape the League's governing structure by including religious figures and giving less power to the aristocratic members who had dominated to that point. A Muslim
League Parliamentary Board was formed, including seventeen
'ulama among the fifty-four members. As one of those members,
Maulana Madani took a two-month leave from Deoband and
campaigned tirelessly for the Muslim candidates. In the United
Provinces alone the League did well. On the whole, however, the
League drew a mere 5 percent of the total Muslim vote. It was
particularly weak in Bengal and Punjab, each dominated by regional
parties that were defined by economic rather than religious interests.
As for Congress, its triumphs were stunning, winning all of the
general seats, some 758 of 1500, in the provincial legislatures, and
forming ministries in seven provinces.

The aftermath of the elections marked a decisive break for the
future of political negotiations in India. The League had expected to
form a coalition with Congress in the United Provinces, but with
their own majority in place, the Congress disdained cooperation
unless the League essentially dissolved itself into the Congress. At
this point, the humiliated League leadership turned to its own "mass
contact" campaign, as did the Congress, each trying to enroll individual Muslim members. Even though the League program subsequently diverged so sharply from that of Congress and its

associates, this brief alliance serves as a reminder of how much all nationalists had in common in their opposition to British control as well as in specific policies that accepted the colonial sociology that India was made up of a mosaic of religiously defined groups.

From the end of the Ottoman Khilafat in 1924 until this point, the "westernized" Muslim leadership and the Jamiat had moved in parallel, opposing colonial rule and seeking safeguards for Muslims against Hindu "majoritarianism" in various constitutional proposals. But the Jamiat in these years was also concerned with a range of Islamic issues, like the bill to appoint Muslim *qazis* to adjudicate personal law, which Muslim League leaders either opposed or ignored (Hardy 1971: 76). The rejection of the positions of the *'ulama* on matters like these made the nominal Muslim political leaders of the League less acceptable to the Jamiat than the Congress leaders, who deferred to them as part of their program of cultural pluralism and minority rights.

Not only, however, had the League reneged on promises to defer to the *'ulama* on religious matters, but they had refused to distance themselves from the aristocratic figures who dominated their councils. Writing in the late 1930s, Maulana Madani identified himself and his colleagues not only as Islamic leaders but as progressives – *taraqqi pasand* – and Jinnah as someone who, from the time of the Khilafat Movement and the first non-cooperation movement on, had favored reactionaries and aristocrats, a grievance that Nehru and others in the Congress had long underlined. As Maulana Madani wrote to one of his followers, participating in the 1936 election on the side of the League had been an opportunity to oppose the National Agriculturalist Party of landlords and also to advance the possibility of a strong Muslim political voice. But when the election was over, Jinnah ignored the opinion of religious leaders on a series of bills on matters of personal law that came before the legislature. When challenged about reneging on his promise to replace the reactionaries with religious leaders, Jinnah had simply replied that that promise had merely been "politics." In Madani's opinion, Jinnah's flawed character had been revealed (*Maktubat*: I, 358–361, 384). Issues of character had thus been added to issues of policy and class.

DEFENDING "COMPOSITE NATIONALISM"

In the aftermath of the election, the claim of the Muslim League, with Jinnah as its mouthpiece, to be "the sole spokesman" for India's Muslims intensified. The League, moreover, increasingly articulated demands for Muslim geographic autonomy. Maulana Madani, in contrast, ever more clearly formulated his arguments for Muslim and non-Muslim politicians to work together under the aegis of the Indian National Congress. In late 1937, he found himself immersed in a controversy that culminated in his most influential writing, *Muttahida Qaumiyyat aur Islam* ("Composite [or United] Nationalism and Islam"), his Islamic justification for a secular government for a society comprised of people of varied religious backgrounds.

The occasion was an ostensible misunderstanding picked up by the failing, but still acerbic, poet Muhammad Iqbal. The "misunderstanding" made clear the fundamental cleavages that had emerged in thinking about the future of Muslim political life in the subcontinent. In December 1937, at a political meeting in Delhi, Maulana Madani made a straightforward statement: "Nowadays, nations (*qaumeen*) are based on territorial homelands (*autaan*, pl. of *watan*), not religion (*mazhab*)." What made this point obvious to him was that people abroad made no distinction of whether a person was "Muslim, Hindu, Sikh, or Parsi" – all were viewed as "Hindustani." By the next morning, the Urdu newspapers *al-Aman* and *Ehsaan* (soon followed by others across the country) had reported that Maulana Madani had said that *millat*, a term commonly used for *religious* community, derived from homeland.

Madani had not said that, but the report provided Iqbal an opportunity to insist that Muslims needed a political unit or units of their own. His reply consisted of three vitriolic Persian couplets:

> The non-Arab ('*ajam*) *still* does not know the secrets of the faith
> Thus from Deoband Husain Ahmad proves somewhat strange
> Singing out high on the pulpit
> > That *millat* is based on land (*watan*).

What does *he* know of the stance of the Arab Messenger, on whom
    be peace?
Bring yourself close to Mustafa, for his alone is faith complete
If you cannot approach him
                                    You're just an Abu Lahab!

This was a scandalous poem. It suggested first of all that Maulana
Madani as a non-Arab did not know Arabic – and this about
someone for whom mastery of the classical Arabic disciplines was the
core of his life's work. Second, it mocked Madani's political role,
placing him on a "pulpit" – and "singing" – when in fact he had been
addressing a public meeting. Perhaps worst of all, it implied that .
Maulana Madani, whether spiritually or in terms of behavior, was far
from the Prophet.

In mock sympathy, Iqbal changes his tone in the last verse to give
kindly advice to him to change his ways and then makes the deadly
riposte that, if he does not, he is "*just an Abu Lahab!*" – the "Father of
the Flame," the nickname for the Prophet's uncle who rejected his
prophecy and was consigned in the Qur'an "to roast at a flaming fire"
(Sura CXI). Abu Lahab's name is a byword for Arabic linguistic elo-
quence coupled with the greatest moral/intellectual failure any
human can make, the rejection of the Prophet of Islam. Thus, even if
Maulana Madani *did* know Arabic, it counted for little. Since Maulana
Madani was in fact a master of Arabic and Iqbal was not, Iqbal was
undercutting an obvious criticism of his own authority before it was
even made.

Verses from the great poet, Maulana Madani's response, Iqbal's
reply, a second round, and then Madani's book all made for headline-
grabbing news and further dissemination of the exchange in reprints
and pamphlets across north India and especially into Punjab. The
poem lived on, reprinted in Iqbal's posthumously published final collection of poetry. For many, the debate was reduced to a fundamental difference about the basis of political community in general –
territory or religion – and the choices now seemingly placed before
the Muslims of India.

Iqbal himself, however, had a far more profound disagreement with Maulana Madani, for he denounced in any form the modern, territorially based nationalism modeled by Europe. He believed that the nation was destructive of ideal human relationships as symbolized by Islam (Iqbal 1973: 234–235). In poetry and prose, in company with a minor strand of other Indian intellectuals like Rabindranath Tagore (1861–1941), as well as with other European and non-European critics across the globe, Iqbal denounced the "black" side of modernity particularly evident in the wake of the Great War: competitive nationalism and its resultant militarism, imperialism, and consumerism. Nationalism, he also believed, inevitably led to indifference toward religion, as had happened in Europe, the reduction of religion to "a merely private affair" (Iqbal 1973: 235). As he wrote in his response to Maulana Madani, "I have been repudiating the concept of Nationalism since the time when it was not well-known in India and the Muslim world" (Iqbal 1973: 230).

Iqbal, unrealistically, struggled to imagine a world in the twentieth century *with no nationalism at all*. He thought that Muslim political autonomy would foster in one place a less divided and less exploitative society on the basis of an Islamic moral system that would in fact serve all people, Muslim or not. Just as Madani saw the hand of imperialism in breaking apart *religiously* plural societies on religious grounds (as Muslims and Christians) in the Ottoman Empire, Iqbal emphasized European intervention as severing *ethnically* distinct Muslim groups (Arabs and Turks) who should have seen their common bonds in the lofty ideals of Islam. The Prophet, he argued, rejected those of his own lineage – like Abu Lahab – who denied Islam. He was not a nationalist leader but a leader of co-religionists (Iqbal 1973: 242–243).

In concluding his statement, far from glossing over the differences between them, Iqbal went beyond the insult of his original verse. He went so far as to identify the ideas of "Maulana Husain Ahmad and others who think like him" as being as egregiously deviant as those of the modern sect, the Ahmadiyya (or as he called them "Qadiani").

The Ahmadis were alleged to deny the fundamental Islamic tenet of the finality of the Prophet Muhammad. The idea of territorial nationalism might be political, Iqbal wrote, and the idea of prophethood theological, but both positions, he argued, transgressed "what the divine law [had] prescribed and defined for them for all time to come." This was a low blow indeed.

For Iqbal, Islam was a "spirit" whose custodians were properly not the *'ulama*, for whom Iqbal for the most part had little respect, but creative individuals like himself, without "priesthood and hereditary kingship," given "the constant appeal to reason and experience in the Qur'an, and the emphasis that it [laid] on Nature and History as sources of human knowledge" (Iqbal 1973: 126). This vision stood apart both from the traditionalist orientation toward fidelity in individual practice of *'ulama* like Maulana Madani as well as from the totalizing Islamist ideology that would organize an Islamic system in all dimensions of life, the ideology associated with Maulana Maududi. That the seed Iqbal watered with these remarks would grow into the virulently nationalist state of Pakistan is surely one of the great ironies of twentieth-century history.

Maulana Madani in reply did indeed proceed exactly as a traditional scholar would. He entitled the first substantive sub-heading of his book: "The key to Qur'anic vocabulary and the words of Hadith will come only from the Arabic tongue" (Madani 1938: 7). Approximately the first half of his treatise then proceeded to a meticulous examination of texts, provided both in Arabic and in Urdu translation, scrutinized in the light of Arabic usage as known from grammars and dictionaries of the Prophet's own time, in order to deny what he saw as Iqbal's equation of *qaum* and *millat*. He established that in the Prophet's usage a *qaum* could consist of believers and unbelievers who both act together for a common purpose – and that would be the model for the *qaum* of India. His medium was central to his message as he displayed the Arabic-based knowledge that asserted his authority.

A second theme that Maulana Madani set out was his insistence, against Iqbal's criticism to the contrary, that his position better served Islam. He fully embraced the classic belief that Islam was intended for all humankind. In his own sub-heading, he equated this universal audience with the "intrinsic" or "inner" (*ma'navi*) meaning of "*qaumiyyat*" (Madani 1938: 22). All people within the Indian *qaum* may not, to be sure, accept this Islamic message, but in the larger context of undivided India, it would be available to all (Madani 1938: 23). Moreover, however committed he was to Indian nationalism, he confirmed that the bonds among those who followed Islam were indeed the basis for the greatest unity among humans that could exist.

And third, Maulana Madani returned to the machinations of the colonial rulers in fostering divisions of race (*nasl*) and homeland (*watan*) in Ottoman lands as what he feared would happen again with the division of India. To do this, the duplicitous British praised nationalism raised against the Ottomans but subsequently deplored it when it united Hindus and Muslims in India under the pretext of concern for the safety of Muslims. For Madani, Muslims and non-Muslims already worked together, needed to continue to work together, and, in the spirit of the Constitution of Medina, in the new state would bind themselves to each other even against a common Muslim foe. Muslims should not, he argued, fear Hindus but only the British whose interests alone were served by the movement for Partition. To underline this, he ended his pamphlet with his own Persian verse, this one of warning to those "dupes," as he saw it, who favored separation:

"I fear that you will not reach the Ka'ba, O desert Arabs!
The path you tread is [in fact] the one to England!"

Maulana Madani was not the first nationalist to invoke the Constitution of Medina as precedent for the alliance with Hindus in the struggle against Britain and the proposed independent state. Maulana Azad had cited this model as early as 1913, in his Karachi address to the Congress, as an occasion to identify Hindus as those "unbelievers" with whom Muslims shared common interests and ought to ally, in contrast to the British unbelievers who brought harm. As noted above, Maulana Anwar Shah Kashmir, in 1927 at the annual meeting of the Jamiat Ulama, had similarly stressed the same three key points: the prophetic precedent of alliances with trust-worthy non-Muslims, the integrity of Muslims in keeping their pledges, and the long historical ties and love of country of the Muslims of India (Anwar Shah 2004). Maulana Madani, thanks to his encounter with Iqbal and his longevity, was central in making the basic Islamic argument for common nationhood widely known, especially through the networks of the Urdu-speaking Muslim elites, and in doing so with a scholarly apparatus that commanded respect.

Maulana Azad serves as an instructive contrast to Maulana Madani as someone who like him was fully committed to an undivided India but whose intellectual justification of this stance diverged from his in significant ways. Azad had received an Islamic scholarly education from his father, but he also had learned English, knew the works of Sayyid Ahmad Khan (1817–1898) and other modernist thinkers, and had also read influential thinkers based in the Middle East like Jamal al-Din al-Afghani (1838–1897) and Rashid Rida (1865–1935). He was one of the founding members of the Jamiat Ulama-i-Hind, and he embraced non-cooperation enthusiastically. In relation to the Khilafat Movement, in contrast to Maulana Madani who emphasized colonial *realpolitik* at the expense of Muslims, Maulana Azad theor-ized the legitimacy of a universal government as an earthly analog to theological *tauhid* (Divine Oneness). Within India, he was active in encouraging the establishment of extra-governmental Islamic courts throughout the country, initially in the context of non-cooperation, but ultimately as a building block for the future free nation (Ghosh 1997). He even imagined India's Muslims under an *amir*, a leader like himself who would guide and speak for Muslims within the larger society. The practical contradictions of his early vision of a modern state coexisting with a universal *khilafat* were resolved by the aboli-tion of the *khilafat* and his own reconsiderations.

Also distinctive in these years was Azad's attempt to find a theo-logical justification for the truth claims of other religions, again, an undertaking far more speculative and all-encompassing than

Maulana Madani's more pragmatic political thought. His key concept was a theory of *wahdat-i adyan*, "unity of all faiths," an ecumenicism that saw a common core in all religions and made religion as much as anything an inward, aesthetic experience. Such an understanding evokes strands in Gandhian thought. Azad, however, wrote very much for an elite, and to the extent that his ideas were known, they proved very controversial.

As early as 1922–1923, however, there was what the critic Aijaz Ahmed calls "a monumental shift" in Azad's orientation. Increasingly, he sought to project himself not only as a leader of Muslims, but rather as a leader of the national movement as such, even as he was always pegged as representing Muslims within the Congress. By the mid-1930s, he had completely abandoned his theological writings. By 1940, when Azad delivered the presidential address at the annual Congress meeting at Ramgarh, one of his best-known and most quoted statements, he had come to a wholly *secular* form for argumentation in order to assert that Muslims were an integral part of Indian society because of their shared history and culture:

> Eleven hundred years of common history have enriched India with our common achievements. Our languages, our poetry, our literature, our culture, our art, our dress, our manners and customs, the innumerable happenings of our daily life, everything bears the stamp of our joint endeavour. There is indeed no aspect of our life which has escaped this stamp. Our languages were different, but we grew to use a common language; our manners and customs were dissimilar, but they acted and reacted on each other and thus produced a new synthesis. Our old dress may be seen only in ancient pictures of bygone days; no one wears it, today. This joint wealth is the heritage of our common nationality and we do not want to leave it and go back to the time when this joint life had not begun [Azad 1940: 237].

In this speech, Maulana Azad meant by "composite culture" a shared culture, not a mosaic. The dimensions of that shared culture, moreover, were ones that could be labeled secular or cosmopolitan. Maulana Madani agreed on these commonalities, and even on occasion spoke of them himself, but his own work emphasized the heritage that made Muslims distinct. Nonetheless, both thinkers justified a political model, unknown in the pre-colonial past, in which no religious tradition was privileged and citizens cooperated as equals – even as precedents of a sort were identified from the Islamic past.

DIFFERENCES: AGAINST THE *'ULAMA*, AMONG THE *'ULAMA*

Although the best-known Muslim opponents of the nationalist *'ulama* were associated with the Muslim League, there were others. Two of those deeply opposed to the leadership of the *'ulama* began to attract attention in the 1930s. 'Inayatullah "Mashriqi" offered a socially radical, fascist-inspired movement, the Khaksar, based in the Punjab but with a presence elsewhere in north India from about 1930 on. Mashriqi offered his own solution to the problem of religious pluralism with a vision of Islam wholly un-moored from ritual practice and meant to include virtually anyone sympathetic to his program. Authoritarian, paramilitary, defiant of the legitimacy of the *'ulama*, Mashriqi clashed with both Ahrar and Congress and increasingly came under the influence of the Muslim League. Less socially extreme, but ultimately far more influential, the emerging "Islamist" vision of Abul A'la Maududi was yet to take any institutional shape, but he condemned both the pluralism of the Congress vision and the secular state imagined by the Muslim League. He broke with the traditionalist heritage in favor of the direct interpretation of texts favored by the modernists. Both of these movements were very much part of global styles of politics in the interwar period (Daechsel 2006).

Maulana Madani did not much take the Khaksar into account, but he wrote frequently against the ideas of Maududi. As early as 1939, he replied to an inquirer that Maududi was not worthy of attention. After all, he explained, just as a person without a law degree had no credibility in a court, neither should someone like "Abul A'la Sahib, a journalist and writer of articles and editorials" be expected to render *fatwas*, no matter how sincere or dedicated to Islam he might be.

To the same writer, he also commented about his fellow Deobandi of a slightly older generation, Maulana Ashraf 'Ali Thanawi. In contrast to Maududi, he wrote, whatever their substantial political differences, Maulana Thanawi was a distinguished scholar, vastly experienced, a writer whose contributions had brought light to the world (*Maktubat*: I, 402–407). Maulana Thanawi throughout the period of mass political activity following World War I had continued to insist that the role of the *'ulama* was to focus on teaching and guidance, not on political activism. Given the disproportionate power still held by the colonial rulers, he believed, such activity put the relative freedom that Muslims enjoyed at risk. Suspicious of the Hindu idiom of much in Congress activities, by the late 1930s, he came reluctantly to recommend support for the Muslim League (Zaman 2008: 39–56). Although Maulana Thanawi died in 1943, before Partition, he is commonly regarded as a spiritual supporter of the Pakistan movement.

The distress among the followers of the *'ulama* at this mounting divergence led Maulana Muhammad Zakariyya (1898–1982), Maulana Madani's counterpart as *shaikhul hadith* at Deoband's sister school, the Mazahirul 'Ulum in near-by Saharanpur, to write a book on the subject of the differences between Maulana Thanawi and Maulana Madani. He framed the book as answers to questions posed in a long letter from one of his own followers. The key question was how it was possible that there could be such deep differences between two such saintly men. Maulana Zakariyya's reply reflected the fact – stereotypes about Islamic rigidity to the contrary – that traditionalistic Islamic reasoning, operating as it did from identifying moral guidelines for specific contexts, often yielded different opinion. Differences among the great and authoritative, he wrote, were at the heart of Islamic guidance throughout history (Muhammad Zakariyya 1938: 1–2). Indeed, Zakariyya had written an earlier (unfinished) book spelling out the differences of the *imams* of the four classic Sunni law schools, all of which are considered legitimate but reach different rulings despite being based on the same texts and utilizing the same disciplines of *hadith* scholarship and law (Muhammad Zakariyya 1928–1929). Maulana Zakariyya took the position, despite the escalating tensions and even violence over allegiance to Congress or to the Muslim League, that the differences between Maulanas Madani and Thanawi were in fact minor. As he wrote to the inquirer:

> As for the disagreement [over politics] being of tremendous depth [as the questioner had suggested], I say that I do not consider the differences to be strong at all. All I can say is that the present political situation causes temporary disagreement. One person's view is that joining the Muslim League is beneficial for the Muslim Ummat and that to join the Indian National Congress is to their disadvantage, the other person on the other hand believes sincerely that the opposite is true [Muhammad Zakariyya 1938: 3].

Maulana Zakariyya directed his readers to simply support whoever, in his opinion, followed "the better path." For someone who felt unable to reach an informed opinion, Maulana Zakariyya urged the person, if possible, to opt for the one whose charisma was greater: "he should stay in the presence of these persons for a couple of days. Thereafter, whomsoever of the two he feels himself drawn to most strongly, he should follow" (Muhammad Zakariyya 1938: 3). In the end, the quality of the person himself was decisive, a standard that gives added meaning to Maulana Madani's public rupture with Jinnah on the grounds that he had lied. Substantively, the positions of Madani and Thanawi were in fact not that far apart: both shared the historic premise that the religious and political spheres were essentially separate and that society was comprised of religiously bounded "communities." Both believed, most fundamentally, that the traditionalist *'ulama* – not the modernist, not the Islamist – alone spoke for Islam and alone were entrusted with the Islamic education and guidance that were at the heart of Muslim well-being.

THE SHI'A–SUNNI DISPUTE IN LUCKNOW

In these years there were innumerable flashpoints where various loyalties intersected with political alignments. In Lucknow in the late 1930s, the Jamiat Ulama-i-Hind, with Maulana Madani as president, became embroiled in Sunni–Shi'a disputes that were mired not only in sectarian difference, but also in League and Congress competition, as well as contestation with official regulations. Maulana Madani in his written statements addressed only this last issue, an example of his ongoing opposition to the colonial state, presenting the Jamiat's intervention in Lucknow as a form of non-cooperation, not sectarian controversy as such at all. If nothing else, the event shows the extent to which he had internalized a language of rights and of "religion" as a domain entitled by the colonizer's own values to resist government control.

The problem went back to a colonial decision in 1908 intended to restrict proclamations offensive to each sect. On the Shi'a side, the proclamation was the *tabarra*, or ritual cursing of the first three caliphs who, the Shi'a believed, had usurped the rightful place of the Prophet's nephew and son-in-law, Imam 'Ali. On the Sunni side, it was the *madh-i sahaba*, ritual praises of those same three successors. Under the terms of the long-standing colonial regulations, the Sunnis were prohibited from uttering these praises during processions on three specific calendrical dates deemed especially sacred to the Shi'a. In the 1930s, voluntary organizations were active on both sides to test these restrictions.

The Deobandis, to be sure, had long denounced the Shi'a practices, especially those associated with the mourning month of Muharram, that they believed had unduly elevated the *imams*. Maulana Madani, however, aside from the conflict stimulated by Ahmad Riza Khan's campaign early in the century in the Hijaz, had not particularly participated in the intra-Muslim debates that engaged many in this period, except for his controversies with Iqbal and Maududi stimulated by their opposition to the larger nationalist movement. Others of Madani's Deobandi colleagues, like Anwar

Shah Kashmiri, were well-known, for example, for anti-Ahmadi writings. Maulana Madani in fact, soon after his return from Malta, as noted above, had stopped in Amroha during the first non-cooperation movement specifically to persuade Muslims to avoid a Sunni–Shi'a confrontation in favor of forging a joint front against the colonial government (*Naqsh-i hayat*: II, 264–265). His intervention in Lucknow thus seemed a reversal of his earlier role.

In 1937, the United Provinces provincial government appointed a commission consisting of two British civil servants to adjudicate the continuing Sunni–Shi'a contestation over the restrictions. Both in his testimony to the commission and in a letter to the chairman of the Sunni organization active in the dispute, Maulana Madani presented the Sunni side as an objection to government interference in what was an incumbent obligation, indeed its performance a legitimate right, which he specified as a "religious," "human," and "civil" right, namely, to praise one's own religious leaders. In contrast, moreover, both by India's criminal code and international law, he argued, no one had the right to denounce the leaders of another religion (*Maktubat*: III, 170–177). Maulana Madani thus demonstrated, as he did regularly, his immersion in the public discourse of colonial society. Excerpts from his letter appeared in newspapers and on posters throughout the province.

Maulana Madani and the Ahrar leader, 'Ata'ullah Shah Bukhari, subsequently came to Lucknow to support the Sunni side in testing the restrictions (Asir Adrawi 1987: 254–255). Meanwhile, Muslim League supporters and militant volunteers of the Khaksar were arriving in Lucknow, hoping to discredit the Congress ministry, whom they accused of dividing Muslims in order to control them. The All-India Shi'a Conference had long since allied with the Congress, and Sunnis, for the most part, had supported the League (Chander 1987). Thus Congress and Ahrar support for the Sunni side in the dispute potentially put Sunni support for the League at risk. In April 1940, a Shi'a attack on a Sunni procession resulted in a police firing and the loss of several lives (Ahmed 1983: 343), a grim event in a decade whose horrors would only grow worse.

TRANSITIONS

In these years, Maulana Madani also faced the death of his third wife and, in 1936, he concluded a marriage with a cousin's widowed daughter. As he explained in a letter to a friend, the age disparity, given that he was now sixty and the woman only twenty-two, seemed extreme, but the family, despite repeated efforts, had failed in finding a match, presumably because of the old stigma among elite Indians forbidding widow remarriage. Madani said that if the woman and her mother agreed to this proposal of male members of the family, he would agree, and the marriage was indeed celebrated. In the letter, Maulana Madani reported that his wife got on well with his son Asad (1928–2004, who would in due course succeed his father as president of the Jamiat Ulama). Asad, he wrote, no longer missed his mother (*Maktubat*: I, 134–136). In 1939, for the first time since his dramatic departure from the Hijaz in 1916, Maulana Madani returned to Mecca and Medina, where he met his family, completed the *hajj*, and was honored by the sultan (Rizvi 1980: 228).

The war years for India ushered in the final stage of the nationalist struggle. With the outbreak of war in 1939, the Viceroy, without consultation, proclaimed India's support for the Allies. At this arrogation of power, the Congress provincial ministries resigned. The Jamiat Ulama's own resolution declared that they could find no reason to support a war that furthered Britain's aims. Jinnah, in contrast, proclaimed Muslim League support for the war effort, a position that enhanced his standing with the colonial government and allowed the League to further establish its base, especially after 1942, when the Congress leadership was largely returned to jail. The end of the 1930s found Maulana Madani campaigning on behalf of Congress not only within his own province but as far east as Bengal and Assam, where his deep ties dated from the time of his return from Malta, and as far into the northwest as the Frontier, where British sources reported his movements as late as 1939 (L/PS/1760. Political (External) Department. 1939). As president of the Jamiat Ulama, he delivered presidential addresses in 1940 and 1942, the latter the prelude to his own arrest and imprisonment in July. In these years Maulana Madani fought with every weapon at his command – tours, letters, publications, negotiations – for what was, in the end, the unsuccessful cause of a united India.

6

"THE GLORIOUS WARRIOR": AGAINST BRITAIN, AGAINST PARTITION

In March 1947, with religious violence already flaring up in the northwest and the timetable for Partition in place, Maulana Sayyid Muhammad Miyan, an active member of the Jamiat Ulama and a devoted disciple of Maulana Madani, published a pamphlet on Maulana Madani's life entitled *Mujahid-i Jalil*, "The Glorious Warrior." The pamphlet was written in response to an extensive campaign against Madani on the part of Muslim League sympathizers. The pamphlet was not about politics; it was about Maulana Madani's superior moral character. A person whose ethical and spiritual standing was unparalleled was engaged in what was nothing less than a *jihad*. It was such a person whom the critics had made the target of thousands of slanders and vilifications for which, Muhammad Miyan warned, these "self-proclaimed Muslims" should remember that they would one day, before God, be called to offer proof (Muhammad Miyan 1947: 17).

As described by Muhammad Miyan, Maulana Madani in these final years before Independence was traveling half the time to bolster the efforts of various religious and nationalist organizations in their political work. When he was in Deoband, he sustained as well another side of his *jihad*, preparing a new generation of scholars to master, embody, and disseminate reformed, traditionalist teachings.

Muhammad Miyan portrayed a life of extraordinary discipline. Maulana Madani arose before dawn for the first prayer, followed by an hour of Qur'an recitation and study. He then breakfasted with any guests before teaching the seminary students and carrying out his obligations as principal until noon. After lunch, a short nap, and the noon prayer, he dealt with mail and met additional visitors until the afternoon prayer, and then would promptly return to his *hadith* classes until the sunset prayer, followed by an hour of supererogatory prayers. He would dine with guests until the time of the night prayer, at which point he would commence a three-hour class on Bukhari Sharif, one of the primary texts of *hadith*, typically attended by about 250 Indian and foreign students. He regularly performed the extra late-night *tahajjud* prayer and used those quiet hours for *zikr* as well. Many readers of the pamphlet would recognize even from the schedule that Maulana Madani modeled the life of the Prophet.

His role as teacher and spiritual guide reached well beyond the walls of Deoband. He wrote constantly in these years – letters, pamphlets, speeches, and a book. He wrote while traveling on the train; he wrote in jail, even when it was against orders – smuggling out letters referring to himself in the third person (*Maktubat*: IV, 88–89; 47). In Moradabad jail in 1942, he taught sessions for his fellow political prisoners until the class came to an end with his transfer to Naini Prison. Thanks again to Muhammad Miyan, notes from these classes were later published as *Dars-i Qur'an ki sat majlisen* ("Seven Sessions of Qur'an Lessons") (Madani 1969). In Naini, Maulana Madani wrote his major text of the period, the two-volume *Naqsh-i hayat*, the narrative of his own life and a history of British colonialism in India. Maulana Madani's published letters from these years show him, as throughout his life, profoundly engaged in the devotional, intellectual, and personal life of his followers. In Maulana Madani's vision, it was Muslims firmly rooted in their faith who would flourish in the independent country of India.

A VOICE CRYING IN THE WILDERNESS?

The first order of political business for Maulana Madani in the years leading up to independence was the continued anti-colonial fight, fueled in part by his outrage at what he saw as Britain's unbridled exploitation of India to support the war effort. By mid-decade, moreover, the threat of the Muslim League to a united India had clearly escalated. In March 1940, the "Lahore Resolution" of the League identified the problems of India not as communal but international. Hindus and Muslims, with their distinctive cultural, historic, and sacred traditions, were said to be separate nations whose problems could only be solved by the division of India into autonomous states. For Madani, this was a disastrous proposal that would in fact endanger Muslims and all Indians, not least by opening the way for continued European manipulation.

Muhammad Ali Jinnah and other League members had been profoundly aggrieved by what they saw as a pro-Hindu bias in the Congress ministries established in 1937, especially the ministry in the United Provinces. Not only were League members excluded from the ministry, but specific policies, like the scheme for basic education, were deemed anti-Muslim. Historians have debated whether the Lahore Resolution was a considered decision to opt for separate states or rather a strategic ploy, aimed above all at shoring up League authority in a "Muslim community" that was in fact deeply divided politically and regionally (Jalal 1995). Either way, it escalated the debate over the fundamental civic identity of Muslim Indians.

Given the denouement of Partition, it is possible to conclude that Maulana Madani in these final years of colonial rule was a voice crying in the wilderness. Nonetheless, he worked tirelessly to fortify an Indian Muslim identity. He continued to comment on the Jamiat plan, described above, for the structure of the independent state. A key to his vision was his expectation, as he wrote in one letter, that the system in a free India would not change much: the only difference would be that Congress members would take the place of the British and be elected to all boards and councils (*Maktubat*: IV, 124–128; II,

115–118). His view, however, increasingly diverged even from that of the Congress leadership in a critical respect, namely their preference for a strong Center as a key to pursuing development and other goals. Like Gandhi with his vision of a weak state and strong villages, Madani never anticipated what the intrusive, developmentalist modern nation state would look like.

Above all, his expectation that Muslims and Hindus would live as culturally contained, relative equals in a united India was not to be. Partition in fact virtually assured that the kind of federated state in which provinces or groups of provinces enjoyed substantial autonomy would not come into reality. Culturally, moreover, Partition set the conditions for nation states to foster the homogenizing *national* characteristics that defined a unified state. India simultaneously gained its freedom and faced the question, so common to the era, of population transfers, refugees, and "minorities" that were not equals but "a problem."

Nonetheless, many of the themes that Maulana Madani propagated in the final years of colonialism continued to be important for India's Muslims after 1947. He demonstrated an informed judgment of the negative impact of colonialism. He accepted religious pluralism among Muslims and Indians generally; he anticipated people working together in all dimensions of life; he approved of Muslims and non-Muslims studying together in secular schools (*Maktubat*: II, 118). He encouraged loyalty to the nation state. And he recognized that the shaping of public opinion was the currency of the secular democratic organization of the united India that he favored.

WORDS AS WEAPONS: ANTI-COLONIALISM, MUSLIM FREEDOM FIGHTERS, SACRED INDIA

If Maulana Madani was a *mujahid*, his only weapon in this *jihad* was words, the range of his armament demonstrated in his impassioned presidential address to the Jaunpur session of the Jamiat Ulama at the beginning of the decade in June 1940. The speech was framed by urgent prayers for God's help and mercy in the wake of the declaration of war, into which India was helplessly drawn, and the continuing cost of India's slavery. He underlined the horrors that the war, with its ghastly new weapons, had unleashed upon the world, and he urged Indians to seek to undermine the British war effort through every form of non-cooperation possible. Indeed, Maulana Madani insisted at Jaunpur that it was in fact a service to the British to oppose their policies – and thus save them from divine judgment.

On this occasion, he invoked at once the common "Hindustani" quality of the inhabitants of Hindustan while noting as well Indians' difference of faith. Such differences, he argued, do not impede national (*watani*) solidarity. He insisted on the rightful place of Muslims within India, given both their heroism as "freedom fighters" and their ancient historical roots in the territory of India (Madani 1990: 41–76; Goyal 2004: 184–190).

Muslims, he added, had a special obligation to anti-colonial nationalism. Here Madani evinced a sophisticated awareness of the crucial place of India in sustaining Britain's worldwide networks. Freedom for India, he argued, would serve neighboring Muslim countries as well as Middle Eastern countries "who have been bound in chains because of India's slavery" (Madani 1990: 73). British policy, moreover, he argued, had been particularly harsh toward Muslims within India since they had suffered disproportionately as victims of the inflation, famine, unemployment, and acute poverty that colonialism had brought. In all these arguments Madani showed a perhaps surprising familiarity with British writers, both those who damned themselves with their own words and anti-colonial writers, many known through Urdu translations in such journals as *Madina*, published from Bijnor. Many were quoted extensively in an influential anti-Muslim League history by Aligarh-educated Tufail Ahmad Manglori (1868–1946), first published in 1937, which Madani often cited, *Musalmanon ka raushan mustaqbil* ("The Bright Future of the Muslims") (Manglori 1994).

Given Britain's intransigence in moving toward the grant of full independence, all Indian citizens, in Madani's view, had to work together in a united front to push toward freedom. In a metaphor that he invoked in the Jaunpur address and on other occasions, he urged people to think of India as a house on fire, or a village dealing with a sudden flood, when all that mattered was that neighbors worked together to avert the crisis. As for Partition, he argued over and over that it would simply allow Britain or other western powers to exercise control and intervene (a prescient observation, one might note, given Pakistan's subsequent role in Cold War and other western alliances). The fact that the Muslim League stood apart from Congress in supporting the war effort only confirmed to Madani the interests of its leadership in currying British favor. In this, he argued, the League and the Hindu Mahasabha were one (*Maktubat*: II, 128–141).

There was an edge to Maulana Madani's emphasis on the exploitation of the British and the contempt they displayed for India's people that was not shared by all nationalists, even those in the forefront of the nationalist movement. As David Cannadine (2001) has argued, the British in India imagined themselves as an aristocracy and cultivated their fellow "aristocrats," among them the princes and specifically the kind of notables who founded the Muslim League. Even someone like Jawaharlal Nehru, who like Maulana Madani stood apart from and deplored the "feudal" interests of the League, had, thanks to his own Cambridge education and polished English, a camaraderie with individual Britons that was outside the experience of someone like Maulana Madani, who argued that Indians had nothing – religiously, linguistically, ethnically, or socially – in common with the British (*Maktubat*: I, 198). Someone like Nehru, in contrast, operated among British officials as essentially an equal.

A second central theme in Maulana Madani's nationalist arguments in these years focused on the central place of Muslims in the history of the emerging nation. Particularly in his 1941 tract "Our India and its Virtues," he pointed out that Muslims had made India their home for over 1000 years, and that in fact most of those now Muslim were descended from earlier inhabitants. Companions of the

Prophet, moreover, had visited India; thousands of scholars, Sufis, and martyrs lie buried in its soil; and India boasts millions of mosques, tombs, and other Islamic institutions. This was the Muslims' ancestral home (Madani 1941). Such claims to early and long residence are characteristic of groups seeking a legitimate or privileged place within a nation. Similarly underlining the territorial importance of nationalism, Maulana Madani insisted that India's Muslims had no greater ties to Muslims beyond the subcontinent than did Hindus to their fellow religionists abroad. This was a response to Hindu nationalist claims that Muslims felt greater loyalty to places outside India, as demonstrated by pilgrimage to Mecca and Medina as well as by their support of the Khilafat Movement.

Madani also contributed to the creation in the interwar years of a specifically nationalist narrative that argued not merely that Muslims were anti-British – but that they were the *most* anti-British. The landmarks of this anachronistic story included an 1803 *fatwa* on the status of India after the British occupation of Delhi in that year; what he described as the anti-colonial *jihad* of Sayyid Ahmad Shahid and others who attempted to carve out a state on the frontier in the early nineteenth century; Muslim peasant movements in early nineteenth-century Bengal; *'ulama* participation in the 1857 Mutiny; and, of course, the conspiracies of World War I that brought him and others to Malta.

Historians have challenged each of these presumed landmarks. The *fatwa* designating India's status as *darul harb* can be seen as a ruling made on technical grounds only to impact such issues as taking interest. The *jihad* was an example of the regional state building of the eighteenth and early nineteenth centuries when such undertakings were, in a sense, the political currency of the day. It was short-lived and unsuccessful, targeted at Sikhs and undermined primarily by other Muslims. The Bengal unrest was fueled by class oppression and was one of many episodes of economic unrest that deployed shared cultural symbols. The 1857 uprising was neither nationalist nor disproportionately Muslim or Islamic. As for the unrest on the frontier during World War I, there certainly were 'ulama like Maulana Mahmudul Hasan who were sympathetic to the endemic resistance on the Afghan border as well as to Turkish and German aspirations to challenge the British on that front. But this was a minor stream of activity for, at most, a handful of 'ulama from the core areas of British India. Nationalists who have written a history of enduring Muslim militancy and conspiracy against the British have often used to their own ends colonial documents that exaggerated "the Islamic threat." Least controversial is the story's final chapter, the history of the Jamiat Ulama, which had indeed both endorsed non-cooperation and stood for complete freedom before even the Indian National Congress had done so.

This historical story was not only a story about Muslim heroism, but specifically a story about the 'ulama. It was therefore also a claim to the recognition that Madani argued was owed to the religious leadership, not the League leaders, as spokesmen for India's Muslims. Muslims under their leadership, he argued, were first to courageously oppose exploitative, tyrannical imperialism. This history of Muslim patriotism was the major subject of the second volume of the *Naqsh-i Hayat*, a work that offers a striking comparison to Jawaharlal Nehru's simultaneous prison writing *The Discovery of India* (1944). Nehru looked for an enduring, distinctive cultural spirit that had imbued the land throughout the ages of history, often resorting to anthropomorphic images as a "civilization" took shape and matured like a human life. The historian Manu Goswami (2004) has argued that there were two central threads in Indian nationalism. One was the focus on colonial exploitation, shading into "autarkic" economic theories that wanted to preserve India's wealth within borders that were increasingly defined and imagined in the course of colonial rule. The second theme was precisely the "organic" one that made the land of India a veritable living being, shading into the powerful nationalist metaphor of India as a goddess, "Mother India." Nehru wrote of himself coming into contact with this reality in his discovery of the peasants of the countryside.

There may seem an irony in the fact that the book of the non-religious lawyer represented this second theme, while that of the

Islamic mystic stressed the first. The Indian nationalist movement was an umbrella for multiple ideologies. The "organic" theme, evident, for example, in the Bengali "Hymn to the Mother," widely embraced by the Congress movement, often proved a problem for Muslim nationalists, while, as Madani himself exemplifies, the hardheaded analysis of economic realities and discrimination was, in contrast, deeply compelling.

Maulana Madani, however, also engaged in some degree of nationalist myth making. In the Jaunpur address and more fully in the following year in the pamphlet "Our India and its Virtues," he traced a mythic history that imbued India with Islam in its very essence. The arguments of this pamphlet challenged both those who would cut off the Muslim areas of the subcontinent from the rest of the country and those Hindus who questioned the right of Muslims to be there. Maulana Madani appropriated an old genre of Arabic travel literature, *faza'il*, to jump into what might be seen as a competition over the emerging historical myth of nationalism. The Hindu nationalist Vinayak Damodar Savarkar (1883–1966), the intellectual father of today's virulent Hindu nationalism, had written in the early 1920s a widely influential pamphlet, *Hindutva*, arguing that India was a Hindu land, sacred only to Hindus and not to so-called "foreign" Muslims and Christians, who were foreigners whose holy places were not in India at all but in Arabia and Palestine (Savarkar 1988: 293–295). Madani set out to trump Savarkar's claim to India.

Quoting earlier writers in the *faza'il* genre, Madani made several perhaps surprising points. For Muslims, India is in fact, he argued, the second holiest place on earth next to Mecca because Adam descended on Adam's Peak, in Ceylon, after his expulsion from Paradise. It was he who brought from Paradise the astonishing fruits and fragrant plants – "cardamom, clove, kewra, rose, cinnamon, camphor, jasmine, strawberry, ambergris, saffron" – that alone are found in India. He brought tools and cloth, and he may even be buried in India's soil (Madani 1941, 16-20). Since Adam is understood as the founder of the Islamic prophetic tradition, India was the site of the first revelation, the first mosque, the first pilgrimage, and the first

manifestation of "the eternal light of Muhammad." Here, as everywhere, other prophets who taught Islam followed, even if their message was subsequently distorted. "Among various communities
residing in India," Madani wrote, "Muslims alone, because of Adam,
can legitimately claim they are the original inhabitants of the land"
(Madani 1990: 73; Madani 1941: 1).

These were extraordinary arguments given what by the mid-
twentieth century had become for many Indians an unquestioned
historical story. The colonial narrative of Indian history, first formulated in the late eighteenth century, had been to position Muslims as
foreigners, thus making British rule seem less intrusive and, by vili-
fying Muslim rule, more benign. Key elements of that narrative were
appropriated by Indians generally to account for their subjection.
Today, Hindu extremists justify ethnic cleansing on the basis of this
same narrative of Muslims as foreigners.

Maulana Madani made a further, perhaps startling, point about the
Muslim relationship to the land of India, namely that Muslims,
"unlike Hindus and Zoroastrians," did not burn or expose, but rather
buried, their dead. According to their own beliefs, moreover, Madani
continued, Hindus and some other groups of Indians believe that
souls after death take on new forms so that "there is no guarantee that
a Hindu soul . . .will again take birth in India" at all. The grave of a
Muslim by contrast is a place of resort for living Muslims, and a sanctuary till the Day of Judgment. For the dead person, Madani
explains, the "grave is like a Radio Station . . .where messages are
received and transmitted," particularly as others pray and do good
works on behalf of the deceased (Madani 1941: 4–6). This was a dramatic claim that the soil of India mattered profoundly, whatever
Savarkar and his fellows might say, or however readily separatist
Muslims might be prepared to leave the soil of India behind.

Madani in these years also was faced with challenges to his position couched in explicitly Islamic terms. Maulana Maududi's ideas
continued to attract attention. Maududi was very much an auto-
didact, whether of English language and western education or Islamic
texts, and he experimented with a range of political ideologies,

including a stage in the 1920s when he supported the Jamiat Ulama-i Hind and served as editor of their official newspaper. In 1941, he founded a party, Jamaat-i-Islami, to further his "Islamist" aims. Maududi by then was writing in opposition both to the secular scheme of Partition and to the Congress goal of a religiously plural India. The Islamist movements, like Maududi's and the contemporaneous Muslim Brotherhood (started in Egypt), are ones typically led by secularly educated professionals and technical people committed to an "Islamic system," as they call it, parallel to other systems of the twentieth century, such as communism and fascism, that shape all aspects of life: thus, Islamic economics, Islamic society, Islamic governance, Islamic sciences, and so forth. Like them also there is a vision of a highly disciplined "vanguard" of dedicated believers to lead the way. The Islamist movements in principle, moreover, if not in practice, are not nationalist but envision an international system shaped by their principles. Maududi presented himself and his program as both systematic and Islamic (Adams 1966).

In one of Maulana Madani's ringing refutations of Maududi, he argued that theory like his gets you nowhere. "*Siyasiyyat* (politics) is not resolved," he wrote, "through *falsafiyyat* (philosophy)" (*Maktubat*: I, 396). If people fail to pay attention to history and to contemporary constraints, if they hide their eyes from the conditions around them, they are being self-destructive. For Madani, the reality of the day was the anti-colonial and constitutional movement. Maududi's effort to propose "an Islamic order" was abstract and unrealistic.

Maududi routinely denounced the Muslims who supported the Congress on the grounds that a Muslim could not accept the leadership of a non-Muslim. This for Madani was the proof that Maududi lived in a dream world, abstracted from the reality in which the Muslim population of India actually lived. Just think, he wrote, what this would mean. By this argument virtually every Muslim participating in a Municipal Board, or a District Board, or an Assembly, or a Council, or a trade or industrial organization – all of them – would have to resign. Ruin would follow. Muslims with Maududi's vision would also have to live without treatment by non-Muslim doctors, the work of non-Muslim engineers, the buildings of non-Muslim architects, the administrative work of non-Muslim bureaucrats, and on and on.

Second, Madani writes, given that among Muslims themselves there is hardly consensus on religious grounds: just *what* would Islamic rule mean? He provided a list of different orientations (somewhat controversial, since members might resist these labels), what he calls, "Easternism," "Westernism," "Shi'ism," "Qadaniyyat," "Khaksariat," and "Adam taqlid." "Each person," Madani points out, "considers *his* reasoning beyond that of Plato or Socrates" (*Maktubat*: I, 399). It is at this point that Maulana Madani makes clear the extent to which he has internalized the fundamental values of a democratic order: he points out that in a post-colonial country the only sources of authority would be persuasion, guidance, and advice, yet only a draconian state could enforce Islamic conformity given Muslims' own diversity. It is thus clear that Maulana Madani's opposition to Islamist politics did not derive from India's not being a majority Muslim country. Even among Muslims there could be no agreement on the nature of proper Islamic rule nor could a state attuned to the values of the era enforce it.

Madani objected in principle to the assumption that there were Islamic "laws," in the sense of absolute universals that were appropriate in all times and place. Thus he made an analogy between the required canonical prayer, whose rules are subject to individual personal characteristics and contexts (for example, whether a person is sick or well, traveling or staying in one place). Imagine right now, was his argument, how the context of India must impact the choice of political strategy. What dream world was Maududi living in, he implied, to discount the facts of India's mixed and heterogeneous population? How could he imagine enforcing the rules he drew from theoretical premises, like the criminal penalties (stoning, prohibition, or monetary compensation for murder) that were typically enacted by any ruler claiming to be guided by Islamic law? Rules like these, Madani concluded, could not possibly be morally obligatory in India as it was (*Maktubat*: I, 395–401).

Maulana Madani continued to address Maududi's challenges, primarily in responses to letters, throughout the war. His responses to his proposals reveal fundamental aspects of his own political position, in particular his conviction that Muslims would remain, as they were now, divided into multiple sectarian orientations. Moreover, he argued that a state-enforced Islam was unrealistic: in this era, the only route for those who wanted to spread a particular interpretation or practice was persuasion. In the end, Maududi threw his support behind the movement for Pakistan.

Maududi, Iqbal, and Madani presented three distinctive visions of society, reflective perhaps, in part, of the political and demographic variety of India. Maududi, the authoritarian Islamist, grew up in princely Hyderabad where a small percentage of Muslims enjoyed privileged status under the authoritarian Nizam; perhaps this experience facilitated his imagining the role of an Islamist vanguard. Iqbal, the modernist, who envisioned a utopian Muslim polity informed by an Islamic spirit, inherited the westernized, cosmopolitan culture of Lahore, including its strand of romanticism about "the East." At the same time, social injustice in part mapped onto religious difference given the city's dominant Hindu elite amid a Muslim-majority province. Madani's childhood was in the eastern United Provinces, till 1856 under the Shi'a rulers of Awadh. Given the Muslim sectarian divisions of the area, he had no illusions of Muslim unity. Muslims and Hindus were represented at all social levels and they were deeply interdependent. The experience of India for these three figures was not the same.

PROTESTING AND NEGOTIATING THROUGHOUT THE WAR

Anxious to secure India's resources and sustain recruitment to the British Indian Army in order to prosecute its war aims, in March 1942 the British government dispatched Sir Stafford Cripps to head a mission to India to try to negotiate a political agreement. The Jamiat

Ulama passed a resolution arguing that nothing short of complete independence was acceptable and actively encouraged non-cooperation in every form, including strikes and refusal to pay taxes (*Maktubat*: IV, 138–144). A subsequent speech by Maulana Madani led to his arrest in June. The Congress leadership meanwhile had rejected Cripps' offer, focused as it was on constitutional progress at the end of the war. In Gandhi's memorable words, the proposal was "a post-dated cheque" on a tottering bank. In August 1942 an opposition movement across northern India, the "Quit India Movement," brought the greatest crisis of control to the imperial government since the uprising of 1857. The entire Congress Working Committee was arrested.

Maulana Madani was released from prison in August 1944, roughly twenty-six months after his arrest. He clearly had undergone hardships in jail, one incident of bad treatment reaching the newspapers and eliciting an apology, after which there was some improvement in conditions (*Makutbat*: I, 198–205). There were restrictions on reading materials and on visitors. He emerged having lost considerable weight. But he immediately resumed his active role, traveling first to Sylhet, to resume his pattern of spending the month of Ramadan there, and subsequently traveling to gatherings throughout the country.

In May 1945, as the war finally began to come to an end, he delivered a presidential address to the Jamiat Ulama meeting in Saharanpur. This eloquent address, in sixteen precise points, provided a detailed review of the wartime offenses of the "humanity-crushing policy" of the "utterly selfish and merciless" British who, he argued, had left India "half dead." In this speech, he denounced the declaration of war on India's behalf and he spoke in the nation's voice:

> What do I have to do with enmity or friendship, war or peace, with anyone? I am neither Germany's enemy nor friend, nor am I America's . . . I long for one thing, and one thing only, and that is freedom [Madani 1988: 154].

He denounced police firings; imprisonment without trial; abuses under the Defence of India Act, the Army bill, and the establishment of special courts; censorship; the seizure of mills and factories and control of production; the confiscation of grain; the export of trains and engines from India to the detriment of internal travel; shortages of petrol and petroleum; and the tragedy of the export of India's goods through the United Kingdom Commercial Corporation to the Allies "with no concern for the poverty and hunger of India." Alluding to the horrific suffering of the 1943 Bengal famine, he argued that India had deteriorated into a veritable hell. He was outraged by the differential treatment of dissidents in England and those in India. The British were allowed freedom of speech; Indians were not. His remarks were informed by attention to the voice of the "public" as the ultimate arbiter of political life and a defense of "civil liberties" – using the neologism, *huquq shahariyyat* – as a human entitlement (Madani 1988: 154–159). The Saharanpur meeting also reiterated its goals for the future state in what came to be known as "the Madani formula," the arrangements noted above that favored substantial autonomy for the provinces and safeguards to protect minority rights at the Center by some strategy of reservation, requirement of a two-thirds majority of Muslims on any matter impacting them, and an arbitration role accorded to a Supreme Court.

In June 1945 the Congress leadership was released from prison and subsequently met with the Viceroy, Lord Wavell, and the Muslim League leadership at Simla. The very fact of the loyal League presence at Simla, at a time when it had demonstrated neither a minimal electoral base nor the sacrifice of imprisonment, outraged Nationalist Muslims, as they were now called. The talks collapsed with Lord Wavell's acceptance of Jinnah's indefensible insistence that the League be recognized as "the sole spokesman" for India's Muslims, alone entitled to nominate Muslim members for an interim government. With the announcement of elections to be held in the winter months of 1945–1946, the lines were fundamentally drawn for Muslim voters, limited as they were to separate electorates, as a vote for a united India or a vote for Partition.

DIVIDING INDIA

Maulana Madani and the Jamiat Ulama, long focused on the anti-colonial struggle, now faced a campaign against a Muslim opponent. Madani wrote ceaselessly during this critical year, publishing a series of statements against the League with titles like "An Open Letter to the Muslim League," "What is the Muslim League?," and "What is Pakistan?" He emphasized the League's close relationship to the British, and he questioned the League's Islamic credibility as shown by its stance on several legislative bills in the late thirties, including their amendments to the Shari'a Bill, intended to eliminate some customary practices that had been recognized in colonial courts, and their opposition to the unsuccessful Qazi Bill, which the Jamiat had favored to provide for the appointment of Muslim judges to handle key issues of Muslim personal law. It was obvious, moreover, Maulana Madani argued, that the League had no clear vision of the kind of state it planned to inaugurate, with Jinnah and others speaking of a constitution following European models on some occasions; on others, invoking plans for a state modeled on *shari'at*. He pointed to the League's domination by aristocratic classes (*Maktubat*: I, 136; II, 158). And he insisted, based on his own painful experience with Jinnah in 1936, that League promises meant nothing.

In September 1945 the Jamiat Ulama sponsored a meeting of representatives of several Muslim parties: the All-India Momin Conference, whose core membership was the weaver community of Bihar; the Khuda'i Khidmatgar, the Gandhian party from the Frontier; the All India Muslim Majlis; the Ahrar; the Independent Party, which had won half the Muslim seats in Bihar in 1937; and the Krishak Praja Party, which in 1937 had formed a government in Bengal but lost power to the Muslim League during the crisis of the famine in 1943. Together they formed a "Muslim Parliamentary Board" with Maulana Madani as chairman, to contest the election in opposition to the Muslim League.

In November of 1945, the Jamiat faced a particularly painful challenge with the organization of a separate body of *'ulama*, largely

Deobandi, committed to support of the Muslim League. This was the Jamiat Ulama-i-Islam. The leader was Maulana Shabbir Ahmad 'Usmani, who had left Deoband in 1927 to follow Maulana Anwar Shah Kashmiri to Dhabeel but returned in 1935, following his death, as patron of the Darul 'Ulum Deoband. Serious differences soon emerged between him and others at the school, particularly Maulana Madani, because he discouraged participation in political life as a distraction from the core scholarly activities of the students and staff. Shortly after Madani was imprisoned, the crisis reached a peak when sixty students were expelled from the school. Several of Maulana Madani's letters to school staff and elders deplored this on the grounds that the student demonstrations were peaceful and that even at Banaras Hindu University, a school with government support, students were not penalized for political activities (*Maktubat*: I, 346–356; 55–56). Maulana Madani also protested the suspension of staff salaries during incarceration. Staff responsibilities, he argued, included not just imparting education, but serving all needs of Muslims and that was exactly what they were doing (*Maktubat*: I, 331–335).

In 1942 Maulana Shabbir Ahmad resigned from Deoband along with several other faculty members, including Maulana Mufti Muhammad Shafi', the official *mufti* of the school (Rizvi 1980: 240). By the time of the 1945–1946 elections, the Muslim League's campaign, which to this point had been led by secular, constitutionally oriented leaders, now drew decisively on the support of Islamic scholars and Sufis with a rallying cry of Islam in danger.

The Muslim League won all thirty reserved Muslim seats in the central assembly and 442 of the 500 reserved for Muslims in the provinces. The Congress won over 90 percent of the vote in the general constituencies, gaining victory in all the Muslim-minority provinces as well as the North West Frontier. This was an extraordinary triumph for the League. Pakistan had come to mean a modern nation state for India's Muslims, a culmination of decades of constitutional arrangements in which Muslims were shaped as a distinctive interest group with an agenda, goals, and interests in need of protection. Its supporters had also, however, made Pakistan, whose territorial boundaries were not even defined, into a vision of some ambiguous, utopian, Islamic ideal.

Unable to secure agreement between what were now two dominant parties, a "Cabinet Mission" arrived in India on April 1, 1946, to devise a plan for the future state. Maulana Madani attended as chairman of the All India Muslim Parliamentary Board along with representatives from the parties the Board represented. A single page in the official photo album of the Cabinet Mission labeled "Nationalist Muslims" records the presence of five of them: Maulana Madani; Khwaja Abdul Majid of the Muslim Majlis; Mr. Hooseinbhoy Laljee, a businessman and president of the All India Shia Conference; Mr. Zahiruddin, President of the All-India Momin Conference; and Mr. Hisamuddin, President of the All India Ahrars. Maulana Azad, the Congress president, was pictured frequently throughout the album in his distinctive grey *sherwani* and often with a cigarette, but he was not included on this page. The pictures record all but Laljee dressed in *khadi*, and both Madani and Khwaja Abdul Majid wearing the white "Gandhi cap" as well. The penciled queries on the album pages are telling: Is it Madani?; Is Laljee a Muslim? [because he is wearing a suit and tie?]; Is the man labeled "Zahirudin" really Dr. Ziauddin Ahmed? [who was in fact a bearded member of the Muslim League] (A. H. Joyce Collection: Cabinet Mission To India, 1946, Volume 2: Photos 134/2 [12–14]). The Nationalist Muslims, it would seem, were not readily recognized, in Madani's case, in part, no doubt, because he had long resisted being photographed

In their interview with the Mission, the Nationalist Muslims emphasized that the election results were misleading since most of the population, of course, had no vote and many of those who did vote had been misled by their religious prejudices. Zahiruddin, speaking for the Momins and their core weaver constituency, insisted that the Muslim poor, whom he estimated as roughly half the Muslim population, would be far worse off with Partition. Hooseinbhoy Laljee on behalf of his organization registered strong opposition to division on the grounds that it would leave weak units and create unworkable boundaries. He echoed Azad in decrying the separation

A page from the official album of the Cabinet Mission. Maulana Madani is pictured in the upper right corner.

from Hindus of Muslims who for the most part "shared most of the political ideas and dress of the Hindus." Maulana Madani presented the "Madani formula," emphasizing the importance of provincial autonomy, Muslim parity at the Center, an end to separate electorates, and reservations for Muslims (CAB 127/99, Notes of Cabinet Mission meetings and interviews, April 16, 1946).

In fact, the Cabinet Mission proposal included many of these features. It involved a three-tiered federation comprised of three groups of provinces: the Muslim-majority provinces in the east, the Muslim-majority provinces in the west, and a third comprising the provinces of the south and Center. This would be, they thought, a way of meeting the demand for (relatively) autonomous Muslim regions, as well as preserving a single state. For Jinnah, who had throughout repudiated simple democracy in favor of some kind of parity for

Muslims, this solution provided substantially what he wanted, given the size of the eastern and western units as long as Bengal and Punjab remained undivided. But for Nehru, Patel, and others of the Congress leadership such a proposal was unacceptable, not least because it would undermine their goal, in complete opposition not only to the League but to the Jamiat Ulama, of creating a strong central government that could, they believed, pursue policies to further economic development. In July, Nehru repudiated the notion of compulsory grouping of the provinces, and thus this plan, like the earlier ones, was effectively dead. Better an independent Pakistan than a state constrained by strong provinces and by what were seen as the communal and aristocratic interests of the League. The Bengal Hindu Congress leadership saw the division of Bengal as a means to secure their own domination, which then would no longer be put at risk, as they saw it, by the Muslim peasant majority.

Jinnah, desperate to avoid a settlement that would divide the large provinces of Bengal and Punjab and give him the "moth-eaten" Pakistan he had earlier spurned, called in response for a day of "Direct Action" protest in Calcutta on August 16. No one, arguably, could have predicted the ghastly bloodletting that followed, with some 4000 killed. In retrospect, many factors, including the acute economic dislocation, the utter devastation caused by the wartime province-wide famine, and the recent floods of migration into the city, help explain the violence, as does the influence of communalist groups like the Hindu Mahasabha, which had been active in distributing aid during the famine. Some 7000 Muslims were subsequently killed in Bihar as well as large numbers of Hindus in the Bengal district of Noakhali, where Gandhi alone, by his presence, brought some measure of control.

Punjab, where the League succeeded in bringing down the ministry in its own favor, soon also settled into chaos among Hindus, Muslims, and Sikhs. At this point, the British prime minister Attlee announced the appointment of a new viceroy, Lord Mountbatten, instructed to transfer power by June 1948, a date soon moved to August 15, 1947. It was by no means clear what arrangements would be made. Plans included independence for each of the provinces and princely states, who could then unite as they chose, or a united Bengal (floated by Bengali Muslim leaders), or even an independent Muslim Bengal, the denouement that emerged in 1971 after Pakistan's own civil war. Instead the boundary was drawn to define two "wings" of a single Pakistan, divided by over 1000 miles of Indian territory. The Jamiat Ulama-i-Hind essentially stood alone in never agreeing to the plan for Partition, a formal declaration made at their meeting in Lucknow on May 7, 1947 (Goyal 2004: 229).

PARTITION

Maulana Muhammad Zakariyya Kandhlawi, Maulana Madani's beloved younger colleague in Saharanpur, recorded his own experiences of Partition in Delhi and the western United Provinces (Metcalf 1993 and 2004). Maulana Madani would have seen many of the same horrors, and they periodically were together during this terrible time. Maulana Zakariyya was horrified by the hateful and violent slogans and processions in the lead up to August 1947, not least when they began to coincide with what should have been the peaceful and spiritually oriented nights of the sacred month of Ramadan, which began in July 1947. He himself spent that month, as was his custom, at the shrine of Nizamuddin in Delhi where the piety-oriented Tablighi Jamaat movement was based in an adjoining mosque. August 15, the day of Independence, fell on the 27th of Ramadan that year, the sacred date that commemorates the descent of the Qur'an and is typically spent by the devout in prayer and Qur'an recitation.

Maulana Zakariyya wrote that what happened in those days was like accounts in sacred texts of the end of time, when humans would abandon their loved ones, all human relations would be severed, and all normal human behavior would cease. Trapped for four months at Nizamuddin, he survived deprivation, inspections, attempts to force people out of the mosque (which they then feared would be taken over by Hindu or Sikh refugees from Pakistan), and attacks on the neighborhood. One of his most horrifying sights was that of adults at the nearby train station departing for Pakistan, so numb and so reduced to primal survival that they left abandoned children behind. People would gather at the mosque before the trains departed, only to hear Maulana Yusuf, the Tablighi *amir*, tell them in the strongest possible terms that they had to have confidence and not flee Delhi. Maulana Zakariyya himself had told inquirers early on that he was no politician but simply that no place allocated to Pakistan could have the holiness and blessedness for knowledge and spirituality of Hindustan, given the presence of the living and sainted dead and the *madrasas* (Muhammad Zakariyya 1971: 7). When people would arrive at Nizamuddin with a handful of airplane tickets and urge Maulana Yusuf and other elders to leave because they were so desperately needed in Pakistan, Yusuf would say he could not go unless Maulana Zakariyya did. Zakariyya, in turn, said he could not go without the guidance of his two elders, Maulana Madani and the Sufi *shaikh*, Maulana 'Abdul Qadir Raipuri (d. 1963) (Muhammad Zakariyya 1971: 11–13). In the end, some 70 percent of Delhi's half-million Muslim population fled their city in 1947 (Pandey 2001: 124), and even more left later.

During these months Maulana Madani traveled frequently to Delhi from Deoband. The road from Saharanpur to Delhi was completely closed after a massacre, so he would travel by whatever routes at the moment seemed relatively secure (Muhammad Zakariyya 1971: 13–14). On November 12 he managed with great difficulty to get to Delhi, at which point Nehru and Gandhi apparently assigned him a truck with four armed Gurkhas for protection. He proposed to use this vehicle to get the women at the mosque out of Delhi, and an anxious party including Madani, Zakariyya, and a few other men, along with the women, set out on their dangerous trip, made the more so by the fact that the truck broke down twice along the way. Maulana Zakariyya attributed their safe arrival to Maulana Madani's spiritual power (Muhammad Zakariyya 1971: 22–26).

Maulana Zakariyya and Maulana Raipuri were under great pressure to accompany their followers to Pakistan and, a few weeks after this trip, they managed to gather with Maulana Madani for mutual guidance (*mashwara*) in Saharanpur. Maulana Raipuri explained the needs of those who had migrated and the fact that there were other elders still in India as there were not in Pakistan. Hearing this, Maulana Zakariyya wrote, Maulana Madani drew "a cold breath" – a deep, despairing sigh – and, with tears in his eyes, answered: "Our 'scheme' 'failed.' If it had not, there would have been none of this bloodshed or population exchange . . . Now I stop no one from leaving. Although my own home is Medina and [my brother] Mahmud is insisting I come, I am not capable of leaving the Indian Muslims in this wretchedness and mayhem. Whoever is ready to sacrifice his life and goods, honor and respect, religion and the world for Muslims should stay; and anyone who cannot bear all this should just go." Maulana Zakariyya immediately answered that he was with him, and Maulana Raipuri said he could not leave without them. Although Maulana Zakariyya told no one this conversation, and was sure the others did not either, by the time of the afternoon prayer, it was on everyone's lips that "the Three Elders" had decided to stay. Through the blessing of his elders and the grace of God, Zakariyya wrote, those who a day earlier were wracked with anxieties grew calm. Reports of the gathering were widely reported in newspapers, pamphlets, and books (Muhammad Zakariyya 1971: 25–26).

Like others of the Jamiat Ulama-i-Hind, Maulana Madani traveled widely to work to secure peace, but, according to Zakariyya and other observers, he was particularly fearless, trying everywhere to steady the resolve of the Muslims. He sought out those who had sided with the League, assuring them that things would get better and urging them to write to him if they needed help. Not surprisingly, this took a heavy toll on him and at times in the course of a conversation, Maulana Zakariyya reported, he would weep (Muhammad Zakariyya 1971: 31–32). Despite the anguish of these days, Maulana Madani renewed his commitment to the importance of seminary education and general Islamic guidance. *Jihad* against the British and against the League now over, India's Muslims needed to turn their struggle within. This would be the greater *jihad* of moral struggle through personal and community discipline, education, and moral reform.

CONCLUSION: INDIAN INDEPENDENCE AND THE CONTINUING *JIHAD*

The constitutional form that the new India soon adopted enshrined in fundamental ways the secular, democratic political structure that the Indian National Congress and Maulana Madani had long advocated. The central provisions of the religiously neutral state and the rights of religious minorities, including the right to conversion, were in place. Gone were the separate electorates that had long exacerbated communal division. Gone as well, to be sure, was the reservation of seats in governing bodies, an arrangement that the Jamiat Ulama and Madani had preferred, at least as a temporary measure to ensure a Muslim voice. There were now no Muslim-majority provinces, and the percentage of Muslims in the population, instead of some 25 percent, was more like 10. More intangible was the cloud that hung over Muslims, widely blamed for Partition and, as enmity with Pakistan soon developed a military dimension, all too often suspected of ambivalent citizenship.

Maulana Madani was utterly convinced of the centrality of the British hand in the nightmare of Partition, that the colonial power wanted a way to keep the Muslims under their thumb and to weaken India as well. In his presidential address to the Fifteenth General Session of the Jamiat Ulama in Bombay in April 1948, eight months after Partition, he even cited evidence of individual British officers supplying weapons to rioters. He was ready to believe speculation in British papers that disaffected conservatives had even had a hand in Gandhi's assassination three months before (Goyal 2004: 231–232). Whatever the evidence for such a claim, that there was colonial bias and undue official speed in the British pull-out is a fact. To emphasize

Britain's role in a sense served, whether knowingly or not, to try to check the intractable attitude that every Muslim, even those still in India and even those who had fought for a united India, was at some level responsible for Partition. At the same time, for Muslims this message held out hope that with the British gone, and in particular with the pernicious arrangement of separate electorates ended, India's Muslims, shattered and decimated though they were, could face the future with optimism.

In the Bombay address, Maulana Madani outlined guidelines for India's Muslims. Violence had to stop, the heart-breaking violence that had left its "stain on the beautiful forehead of our country."

> To end such cruelty . . . is absolutely central to the "program" of Islam. It is in fact a Muslim's duty to work for this . . . Any suggestion that this . . . violence and killing is "Islamic *jihad*" is a blasphemous slander that mocks [Islamic] teachings . . . [Kamal 2004: 19]

In great sorrow, he spoke of the "most disgraceful and grave event of all this bloodshed, the murder of Mahatma Gandhiji," who was "that true servant of civilization and humanity and real benefactor of the country," his life its greatest treasure, and his commitment to ending communalism its only hope of unity (Kamal 2004: 20–21).

Maulana Madani emphasized that the Jamiat Ulama-i-Hind would now withdraw from politics as an organization and limit itself explicitly to a focus on "the religious, cultural, and educational rights and duties of Muslims." He spoke with admiration of the leadership of Maulana Azad, who was now the Federal Minister of Education, in guiding Muslim organizations in this fraught time. Azad had led the move to disband not only the Muslim League, but all communally focused political organizations. The cultural and educational program that remained, Maulana Madani argued, was an awesome responsibility that fell on each and every Muslim and required co-ordinated efforts in a system of schools, translations, and *shari'a* courts (Kamal 2004: 26–30).

Muslims needed above all, he argued, to concentrate on their own individual conduct and character.

If Muslims want to see their future bright, then it is their duty by their actions and character to prove their importance and usefulness. To the extent that they are useful for the Indian Union, the more respect they will enjoy. In a democratic system, success does not depend on race, religion or family; rather, service and ability is its measure. Cultivate a genuine ardor for service to the country and the community . . . We are not responsible for the Muslims of Pakistan [but only for the Muslims of the Indian Union] . . . To the extent that we plumb Islamic teachings and try to act on them, to that extent we will be the best servants, brave defenders, and an invaluable element in our beloved country [Kamal 2005: 30–31].

Maulana Madani understood a commitment to religious teachings as central to the well-being of India in general.

Muslims, he argued, must not dwell on their minority status or lack of power. Their model must be the small body of the Prophet's followers in Mecca who won hearts not by worldly power but by their actions:

Muslims today remember only the word "*jihad*" but they do not remember that in opposition to rebels against Islam and enemies of the community . . . patience, forbearance, and high ethics were spoken of as *jihad-i akbar* ("the greater jihad"). In this greater *jihad*, there is no need of sword or dagger, but only strength, resolve, and action . . . [Kamal 2005: 32].

Maulana Madani's own *jihad* in his final decades focused on the dissemination of Islamic teachings and practice, coupled with concern for the legitimate place of Muslims in the life of the new India. He continued his administrative and teaching base in Deoband, and he continued to serve as president of the Jamiat Ulama-i-Hind. In that capacity, he addressed several general meetings held in sites chosen to fortify Muslims throughout India, beginning with the Bombay address in 1948 and including Lucknow (1949); Hyderabad (1951), in the wake of the brutal police action to integrate the Muslim-ruled princely state into India; Calcutta (1955); and, his final address, Surat, in Gujarat (1956).

As he had in the Bombay address, Maulana Madani regularly took up many new issues that came with Independence. He called on Muslims to participate in the electoral process as well as in government plans for economic development. He urged them to learn Hindi, the national language. He enjoined the government and ordinary citizens to cultivate good relations, as well as opportunities for trade and travel, with Pakistan, whatever the tragedy of its origins may have been. He expressed his concern with school textbooks that from British times on misrepresented Muslims, an issue that an independent government needed (and continues to need) to address. He called for attention to Islamic endowments, now the purview of state-level governments, calling for uniform laws among the states and oversight to assure fiscal responsibility and appropriate expenditures.

But his primary concern, as the 1948 Bombay address had clearly indicated, was his long-held conviction that Islamic moral and academic education at every level was critical to the life of the Muslim population in India. That certainty was only the greater in the aftermath of what he called the *inqilab*, the revolution, of Independence. The *'ulama* could not look to the state to foster their goals, even, for example, by enacting their long-proposed preference for the appointment of Muslim *qazis* to adjudicate Muslim Personal Law. The *'ulama* had, instead, to continue to struggle to nurture "public opinion," the currency of public life that Madani had long since recognized, in order for individuals to support the particular interpretations and guidance of the *'ulama*. This struggle was challenged, and also stimulated, by the deep sectarian divisions so important in modern South Asian Islam.

Although education was critically the work of the *'ulama*, Maulana Madani was also supportive of the efforts of grassroots teaching represented by Tablighi Jamaat, and he was particularly encouraging in these later years of this apolitical effort to shore up individual faith by traveling in small groups to instruct other Muslims and enjoin them to faithful practice. Many of Maulana Madani's letters from this period encouraged participation in Tablighi activities. The movement had been launched by Maulana Muhammad Isma'il Kandhlawi (d. 1944) in the 1920s, later led by his son Maulana Yusuf, mentioned above in the context of the Partition disturbances, and others based at the Banglewala Masjid in New Delhi. The trauma of Partition marked a critical stage in the scale of the Tablighi Jamaat movement. The anthropologist Shail Mayaram has evocatively shown, for example, how in Mewat, southeast of Delhi, one of the original areas of Tabligh activity, it was only with the harsh "ethnic cleansing" of Partition and the years following that Muslims of the area significantly embraced the more marked Muslim identity encouraged by Tablighi reforms (Mayaram 1997).

These were difficult years. Maulana Madani's consistent message in his letters and speeches was to encourage Muslims to the highest level of morality, patience, and "good for evil." With cooperation from people like Nehru, Azad, and G. B. Pant (the first Chief Minister of the United Provinces), he was able to intervene in individual cases to protect Muslims as well as their sacred sites. He also interceded for some individuals caught up in nightmares of travel between the two countries and issues of evacuee property.

Maulana Madani was not forgotten. Dr. Rajendra Prasad, India's first president, visited the Darul 'Ulum, as did G. B. Pant as well as other ministers. And there apparently was a movement to consider him in 1956 for the national Padma Vibhusan award, a plan he thwarted in a letter to the president, expressing his gratitude but also his concern that such recognition might create the impression that he was in some sense subservient to the government (*Maktubat*: IV, 236–238).

A FINAL STORY

In 1955, Maulana Madani undertook what would be his final *hajj*. On the way home, he visited his followers in Pakistan. The account of a seemingly mundane episode during the course of his travels was

chosen by the editor of his multi-volume collection of letters as one
of his own favorites:

> When Hazrat Maulana Madani returned from his final *hajj* we came
> to the station in Lahore for the honor of seeing him (*sharf-i ziyarat*).
> Among those in relationship with him was Sahibzada Muhammad
> 'Arif, from district Jhang [in Pakistani Punjab], who accompanied him
> as far as Deoband. He reports the following story. On the train, there
> was also a "Hindu gentleman" who experienced a call of nature and
> went to attend to it. Clearly unhappy, he came right back. Hazrat
> Maulana Madani understood what had happened, and immediately
> gathered some empty cigarette packets and a jug of water and went
> and cleaned the toilet completely. Then he said to the Hindu friend,
> "Please go, the toilet is completely clean. Perhaps because it is night
> you couldn't see it properly." The youth said, "Maulana, I saw that the
> toilet was completely full." But he got up and went, and found the
> toilet completely clean. He was much moved and with great
> conviction ('*aqida*) said, "Your honor's (*huzur*) kindness (*bandanawazi*,
> cherishing of servants) is beyond comprehension."

Citing this story, Najmuddin Islahi recalled that a Jewish guest of the
Prophet had dirtied his bedding during the night, and that, "with his
own blessed hand," the Prophet had cleaned it. Islahi took this story
as a sign of the selflessness and self-sacrifice (*be nafsi* and *nafs kushi*) of
the Prophet's own beauty and of Madani's closeness to the Prophet
(Najmuddin Islahi in *Maktubat*: I, 53–55). The story, like others told
above, is a reminder that, to those who heard, there was the absolute
conviction that whatever worldly blows might fall, the model of the
Prophet lived among them and they could focus their own lives on
emulating that model.

The story is also, of course, a story about Hindus and Muslims. Its
structure is that of a Sufi tale (*hikayat*), in which an outsider, even an
enemy, is stunned into recognition of the holy person's charisma. In
the story, Maulana Madani inhabits India with dignity and pride in a
way that is imagined as a metonym for the Muslim community as a
whole. Muslims, like Madani, believed themselves to be the best of

communities; and in the glowing moment of recognition in this story, the humbled and wiser Hindu gentleman accepts the *bandanawazi* of their representative whose worthy and superior status is thus acknowledged. Maulana Madani may appear to be engaged in a humble task but his was the humility of the truly great in a way that was not only timeless but historically specific – the model of the revered and heroic Gandhi who showed solidarity with the humble by cleaning latrines. This is a story for contemporary Indians and Pakistanis, and, from the perspective of Maulana Madani's followers, for the ages.

IN CONCLUSION

Maulana Husain Ahmad Madani stands as an influential and accomplished Islamic scholar and spiritual guide in twentieth-century India. He put knowledge of the great Islamic classical tradition at the center of his life and his work, and he embraced the still new, formally re-organized seminaries, as well as more informal grassroots education, as critical to Muslim life in India. He himself did not engage in polemics but he was, of necessity, identified as a "Deobandi" and thus part of the sectarian identities that came to be so important in South Asian Islam in the last century. He thus participated in the redefinitions, new institutions, and new technologies that contributed to the spread of religious teachings of all kinds during colonial rule. As many of the hundreds of published letters he wrote indicate, he was a humane and attentive mentor to the spiritual and personal problems of those who turned to him for guidance. He left dozens of successors whom he authorized to accept disciples themselves and continue his scholarly and spiritual work.

That work had included Islamic guidance in the fraught context of the final decades of British rule in India. His distinctive contribution to political life was to articulate and disseminate an Islamic justification for forging a common ground with non-Muslims in the struggle against Britain and for envisaging a free nation in which all would live as equal citizens in a territorially defined state. The fact that other Islamic scholars, including ones whom Madani held in high regard, favored a separate Muslim state offers an especially illuminating example of traditionalist legal thought, which, far from rigid, depends on highly contextual argumentation in interpreting the applicability of sacred and scholarly texts. Madani's thought was pragmatic, flexible, and contextual, as was the thought of fellow Deobandis who in the final years of British rule opposed the vision of united nationalism (Zaman 2002: 42–47).

What in Madani's background was decisive in shaping his position? Maulana Madani shared with many of the nationalists, among them Gandhi, in experiencing an identity as "Indian" through residence abroad. In Medina and Malta he was viewed as "Indian." That he acted as an Indian subject in opposition to British rule he himself credited to the influence of Maulana Mahmudul Hasan, who stood apart from many other Deobandis who favored quietism in order to ensure the school's safety, even up to the time of Independence. With Mahmudul Hasan, he observed conditions in Arabia, Egypt (even briefly), and Malta that pointed him toward an awareness of Britain's self-interested strategies on an imperial scale. For over three years on Malta, Maulana Madani identified with a nationally and religiously heterogeneous population united in opposition to the British, and that experience, he himself explained, was foundational for his commitment to working across religious boundaries in India as well.

Mahmudul Hasan died in 1920 during the heyday of activism not predicated on religious community. No matter what happened thereafter, Maulana Madani never deviated from that position. His own travels throughout the length and breadth of India, his particular emphasis on the need to protect India's borders from economic exploitation, and his own foray into mythic writings that sanctified the very soil of India together reinforced his commitment to territorial nationalism defined by the expanse of British India. Even as others feared that Muslims would be marginalized and vulnerable in the new state, he insisted that they had to trust in a future shared with non-Muslim fellow citizens instead of falling prey to a colonialist scheme that would weaken the country, and Muslims, as a whole. Personal qualities no doubt played a role in his adherence to this position, not least a fundamental optimism that allowed him to persevere, a trait honed by long experience in facing and overcoming obstacles.

A central argument of this study has been that Madani's positions need to be understood as an assessment of British rule and, in many respects, a vision of the independent state that were shared with non-Muslim colleagues. Many contemporary critics (not least academics) often deplore the lack of specialized cultural knowledge on the part of today's government leaders in relation to international affairs. There may well be a lesson to the contrary in Husain Ahmad's political positions given that the grievances and goals that shaped his public life were issues of nationalism, economic exploitation, and justice, issues that anyone ought to understand.

A further lesson to be drawn from his life rests in the example he offered of the creativity and relevance of the religious thought of a traditionalist Islamic scholar. As Madani himself said, "The view that Islam is an inflexible religion is beyond my comprehension" (Zaman 2002: 34). In his analysis of Maulana Madani's thought, Peter Hardy has underlined what an extraordinary change from medieval precedents it was to justify *from within the Islamic tradition* the support of equal citizenship and participation in the state with non-Muslims. Moreover, in the goals of the *'ulama*, Hardy points out, the language of the Jamiat Ulama-i-Hind, including Madani's addresses quoted above, was the language of utility, with references to Muslim progress (*taraqqi*) and national and community well-being. The drift of such an argument was, like the demand for Pakistan, as Hardy puts it, "substituting the cultural Muslim nation for the community of believers under God." Moreover, the trend to treating the *shari'a*, he notes, as only an internal moral imperative was, again, a break with the historical tradition (Hardy 1971: 40–42). This understanding that the proper role of the state is to operate without preference to any religion became a pillar of independent India's constitution.

No one else in twentieth-century South Asia had Maulana

Madani's influence in laying out in uncompromising terms the Islamic sanction for Muslims to work and live with non-Muslims in a shared polity, and, specifically, to embrace the secular democracy of a state like India. Certain aspects of his thought were very much products of their times. Like Gandhi, he had little understanding of the emerging developmentalist state. Similarly characteristic of strands in the political thought of the day was his commitment to a system of separate personal laws as well as his Islamic version of a nationalist myth. Nonetheless, Maulana Madani clearly charted a path that has become the norm for Muslims in India, a population notable for its distance from political Islam or even national political organization.

Madani's thought blazed a trail for others. In the Indian context, even Maududi's Islamist Jamaat-i-Islami evolved into an apolitical educational and social service organization, much like the Jamiat Ulama-i-Hind, even as its organization in Pakistan, like Pakistan's Jamiat Ulama-i Islam (the organization that broke away from the Indian Jamiat), became a political party at times sympathetic to militancy (Ahmad 2005). Maulana Thanawi's disciples who found themselves in independent India similarly recognized the value of a secular political framework that secured freedom of religion and administered religion-specific family law. The commitment to democracy and secularism, now realized and justified in over six decades of democratic participation on the part of India's 'ulama and other Muslims, stands as one of India's Muslims' most striking characteristics. Husain Ahmad Madani's legacy of political thought, and his life as a whole, challenge common stereotypes of Muslims generally and of Muslim clerics above all.

BIBLIOGRAPHY

HUSAIN AHMAD MADANI'S WRITINGS

Madani, Husain Ahmad. n.d. *Asir-i malta* ("The Prisoner of Malta"). Deoband: Rashid Kampani. **In references**: *Asir-i malta*

Madani, Husain Ahmad. n.d. [1969?]. Muradabad jel main dars-i qur'an ki sat majlisen: Surah fatihah see muta'aliq irshadat, 'ilmi lata'if, rumuz-i qur'an aur asrar-i hukm ka majmu'a az Sayyid Husain Ahmad Madani wa tashrihat [az] Sayyid Muhammad Miyan ("Seven Sessions of Teachings on Qur'an in Moradabad Jail: A Collection of Injunctions, Learned Stories, and Quranic Secrets on the Surah Fatihah by Sayyid Husain Ahmad Madani and Commentary by Sayyid Muhammad Miyan"). Delhi: al Jami'yyah Book Depot

Madani, Husain Ahmad. [1937] 1973. *Muttahida qaumiyat aur islam* ("Composite Nationalism and Islam"). Delhi: Ekta Trust

Madani, Husain Ahmad. 2008. *Composite Nationalism and Islam*. With an Introduction by Barbara D. Metcalf. Trans. Mohammad Anwer Hussain and Hasan Imam. New Delhi: Manohar

Madani, Husain Ahmad. [1941] n.d. *Hamara Hindustan aur uske fadhail* ("India: Our Land and its Virtues"). Trans. Mohammad Anwer Hussain. New Delhi: Jamiat Ulama-i-Hind

Madani, Hussain Ahmed. 1946. *An Open Letter to the Moslem League*. Trans. Professor Bright. Lahore: Dewan's Publications

Madni, Husain Ahmad. 1951. *Maktubat-i shaikhul islam* ("Letters of Shaikhul Islam"). 4 vols. Ed. and Introduction by Maulana Najmu'd-din Islahi with a Foreword by Maulana Qari Muhammad Tayyib Qasimi et al. Deoband: Maktaba diniyya. **In references**: *Maktubat*

Madani, Husain Ahmad. 1953. *Naqsh-i hayat* ("Impression of a Life"). 2 vols. With an introduction by Maulana Hifzur Rahman. Deoband: Maktaba diniyya. **In references**: *Naqsh-i hayat*

Madani, Husain Ahmad. [1967?] *Husain Ahmad Madani ke chand nayab va ghair matbu'ah khutut* ("Some Rare and Unpublished Letters of Husain Ahmad Madani"). Deoband: Maktuba Nu'maniyya

Madani, Husain Ahmad. 1988. *Intikhab khutbat Jami'yyat 'ulama-i hind* ("Selection of Addresses to the Jamiat Ulama-i-Hind"). Ed. Shuja'at 'Ali Sandilvi. Lucknow: Uttar Pradesh Urdu Akadmi

Madani, Husain Ahmad. 1990. *Jami'yyat 'ulama-i hind ke salanah ijlason men Maulana Husain Ahmad Madani ke salanah khutbat: mas'ala-yi qaumiyyat par Allamah Iqbal se tanazah aur Nehru report par tanqid o tabsirah* ("Maulana Husain Ahmad Madani's Annual Addresses at the Annual Meetings of the Jamiat Ulama-i-Hind: Debate on the Problem of Nationalism with Allamah Iqbal and a Critique of the Nehru Report"). Ed. Ahmad Salim. Lahore: Nigarishat

Kamal, Razi Ahmad, ed. 2004. *Jami'yyat 'ulama-i hind: Dastawizat markazi ijlasha-yi 'am, 1948–2003* ("Jamiat Ulama-i-Hind: Documents of the Central General Meetings, 1948–2003"). New Delhi: Jamiat Ulama-i-Hind

Madani, Husain Ahmad. 2004a. *Shaikhul Islam Hazrat Maulana Sayyid Husain Ahmad Madani: Ek siyasi mutali'a, VI (Silsila-yi maqalat): Maqalat-i siyasiyya* ("Shaikhul Islam Maulana Husain Ahmad Madani: A Political Study, VI (Essay series): Essays on Politics"). Ed. Daktar Abu Salman Shahjahanpuri. Karachi: Majlisi-i Yadgar-i Shaikhul Islam Pakistan

BIOGRAPHICAL WRITINGS ABOUT HUSAIN AHMAD MADANI

'Abdul Wahid Bukhari. 1972. *Shaikhul Islam Hazrat Maulana Sayyid Husain Ahmad Madani: Ek shakhsiyat, ek mutali'a* ("Shaikhul Islam Hazrat Maulana Sayyid Husain Ahmad Madani: A Personality, A Study"). Gujrat. Pakistan: Maktaba-yi Zafar

Abul Hasan A'zami. 1999. *Yah thee Shaikhul Islam Maulana Sayyid Husain Ahmad Sahib Madani* ("That Was Maulana Sayyid Husain Ahmad Sahib Madani"). Deoband: Maktaba Sautul Quran

Abul Hasan Barabankawi. 1975. *Hayat-i Shaikhul Islam Hazrat Maulana Sayyid Husain Ahmad Madani ke hairat angez waqi'at* ("Amazing Episodes from the Life of Shaikhul Islam Hazrat Maulana Sayyid Husain Ahmad Madani"). Deoband: Maktaba Diniyya

Abu Salman Shahjahanpuri, DakTar. 1987. *Shaikhul Islam Maulana Husain Ahmad Madani: Ek siyasi mutali'a* ("Shaikhul Islam Maulana Husain Ahmad Madani: A Political Study"). Karachi: Majlis-i Yadgar-i Shaikhul Islam Pakistan

Abu Salman Shahjahanpuri, DakTar. 2002, 2003, 2006. *Hazrat Shaikhul Islam Maulana Sayyid Husain Ahmad Madan ki siyasi da'iri: Akhbar aur afkar ki raushni men* ("The Political Diary of the Revered Shaikhul Islam Maulana Husain Ahmad Madani: In the Light of Newspapers and Commentary"). 3 vols. Karachi: Majlisi-i Yadgar-i Shaikhul Islam Pakistan

Asir Adrawi. 1987. *Ma'asir-i Shaikhul Islam: Mujahid-i jalil Hazrat Maulana Sayyid Husain Ahmad Madani ki misali zindagi aur karname* ("The Glorious Legacy of Shaikhul Islam: The Exemplary Life and Deeds of the Glorious Warrior Hazrat Maulana Sayyid Husain Ahmad Madani"). Deoband: Darul Muwalifin

'Azizur-Rahman Sahib, Maulana Mufti. 1958. *Anfas-i qudsiyya ya'ni Qutb-i 'Alam Shaikhul Islam Hazrat Maulana Sayyid Husain Ahmad Sahib Madani ki Khasusiyat* ("A Breath of Holiness, i.e. The Merits of the Axis of the World Shaikhul Islam Hazrat Maulana Sayyid Husain Ahmad Madani"). Bijnor: Madina Book Agency

Goyal, D. R. 2004. *Maulana Husain Ahmad Madni: A Biographical Study*. Delhi: Anamika Publishers; published for the Maulana Abul Kalam Azad Institute of Asian Studies, Kolkata

Malik, Rizwan. 1996. "Mawlana Husayn Ahmad Madani and Jami'yat 'Ulama'-i Hind, 1920–1957: Status of Islam and Muslims in India." University of Toronto: unpublished doctoral dissertation

Muhammad Miyan. 1999a. *Hayat-i Shaikhul Islam: Hafiz Sayyid Husain Ahmad Madani Shaikhul Hadis Darul 'ulum Diyoband, Sadar Jam'iyyat 'Ulama-i Hind ke halat-i zindagi* ("The Biography of Shaikhul Islam; The Life Conditions of the Memorizer [of the Qur'an] Sayyid Husain Ahmad Madani Shaikh of Hadith at the Deoband Seminary, President of the Jamiat Ulama-i-Hind"). Lahore: Jam'iyyat Publications

Muhammad Miyan. 1999b. *Asiran-i Malta: Shaikhul Hind Maulana Mahmud Hasan aur Shaikhul Islam Maulana Husain Ahmad Madani aur un ke rufqa ki jidd o jahd-i hurriyat wa azma'ish-i qaid o band ki dastan* ("The Prisoners of Malta: The Tale of the Struggle for Freedom and Trials of Imprisonment of Shaikhul Hind Maulana Mahmud Hasan and Shaikhul Islam Maulana Sayyid Husain Ahmad Madani and their Companions). Lahore: Maktaba Mahmudiyya

Muhammad Mian [Miyan]. 2005. *The Prisoners of Malta (Asira'n-e-Malta): The Heart-Rending Tale of Muslim Freedom Fighters in British Period*. Trans.

Mohammad Anwer Hussain and Hasan Imam. New Delhi: Jamiat Ulama-i-Hind

Muhammad Miyan, Maulana Sayyid. 1947. *Mujahid-i jalil* ("The Glorious Warrior"). Deoband: Kutbkhana islamiyya

Muhammad Zahidul Hasani, Qazi. 2003. *Chiragh-i muhammad: Sawanih hayat qutbul irshad wa'l-takwin shaikhul islam Maulana Sayyid Husain Ahmad Madani* ("The Lamp of Muhammad: The Biography of the Lord of Command and Fulfillment Shaikhul Islam Maulana Sayyid Husain Ahmad Madani"). 3rd edition. Delhi: Al Jamiat Book Depot

Najmuddin Islahi, ed. 1951. "Introduction" to Madani 1951. Vol. I, pp. 14–68

Rashid Hasan 'Usmani. 1957. *Tazkira-i Shaikh Madani ya 'ni Mujahid-i a 'zam, yadgar-i salf, Maulana Sayyid Husain Ahmad Madani ki mujahidan zindagi ke chand pahlu* ("An Account of Shaikh Madani, i.e. Some Aspects of the Warrior Life of the Great Warrior, the Heir of the Ancestors Maulana Sayyid Husain Ahmad Madani"). Deoband: Kutbkhana Rashid Company

BRITISH OFFICIAL DOCUMENTS

The National Archives (Public Record Office), Kew (TNA)
Foreign Office (FO)
Cabinet (CAB)

FO 882/12. Turkey. Arab Bureau Notes on Husain Ahmad and Fellow Internees at Malta, 1917. Turkey. Arab Bureau Papers. 1914–1918

FO 686/149/ff. 202–208. 1916–1917. Jeddah Agency. Papers. Silk Letter Case

FO 371/3046. unpaginated. No. 244943/5414, 29 December 1917. "Visit of Burn to Malta to interview Indian internees." Letter from C. R. Cleaveland, Criminal Intelligence Office (India) to the Hon. Sir James DuBoulay, Member, Home Department, No. 3923/II M.A. Delhi, 1 November 1917

FO 371/3396, ff. 54–58 Turkey. No. 13256, 22 January 1918. Visit of Mr. Burn to Malta to interview Indian internees. F. 57. Mr. R. Burn to India Office, 15 January 1918

FO 686/26: British Agent's political report, 22 May to 1 June 1920
Cabinet Papers: CAB 127/99 (Secret). 1946. Note of interview between
Sir Stafford Cripps and Mr. A. V. Alexander and representatives of the
Nationalist Muslims (Maulana Husain Ahmad Madani, Mr. Zahiruddin,
Mr. Sheikh Hisamuddin, Mr. Abdul Majid Khwaja, and Mr. Hosseinbhai
Laljee) on Tuesday 16 April 1946

Oriental and India Office Collections (OIOC), British
Library, London
L/PS Political and Secret

OIOC. 1946 A. H. Joyce Collection: Cabinet Mission to India, Volume II
Photos 134/2 (12–14)
OIOC. L/PS/10/648: File 287/1917. Arabia: Deportation of
Undesirable Indians, 1916–1920. Statement of Husain Ahmed Madni,
son of S. Habibullah, of Tanda, age 40. 13 December 1917
OIOC. L/PS/648.P.5006/17. Report on Indian Prisoners of War in
Malta. R. Burns. 8 January 1918
OIOC. L/PS/1760. Political (External) Department. 1939. Afghanistan,
The Silk Letter Conspirators

OTHER PRINTED AND ELECTRONIC SOURCES

Adams, Charles. 1966. "The Ideology of Mawlana Mawdudi." In *South Asian
Politics and Religion*. Ed. Donald P. Smith. Princeton: Princeton
University Press, pp. 371–397
Ahmad, Aijaz. 1992. "Azad's Careers: Roads Taken and Not Taken." In *Islam
and Indian Nationalism: Reflections on Abul Kalam Azad*. Ed. Mushirul
Hasan. Delhi: Manohar, pp. 122–155
Ahmad, Irfan. 2005. "From Islamism to Post-Islamism: The Transformation
of the Jamaat-e-Islami in North India." Unpublished doctoral disserta-
tion, Department of Anthropology, University of Amsterdam
Ahmed, Imtiaz. 1983. "The Shia-Sunni Dispute in Lucknow." In *Islamic
Society and Culture: Essays in Honour of Professor Aziz Ahmad*. Ed. Milton
Israel and N. K. Wagle. Delhi: Manohar
Akhtar, Rafique. 1971. *Historic Trial: Maulana Mohamed Ali and Others*.
Karachi: East and West Publishing Company

Anwar Shah Kashmiri. 2004. "Building Bridges of Harmony: A Speech By Maulana Anwar Shah Kashmiri."Trans.Yoginder Sikand. In *Milli Gazette*: http://milligazette.com/Archives/2004/01–15Apr04-Print-Edition/ 011504200459.htm and http://milligazette.com/Archives/2004/ 16–30Apr04-Print-Edition/1604200455.htm

Ashraf 'Ali Thanawi. 1990. *Perfecting Women: Maulana Ashraf 'Ali Thanawi's Bihishti Zewar: A Partial Translation with Commentary* by Barbara Daly Metcalf. Berkeley: University of California Press

Azad, Abul Kalam. [1940] 1988. Presidential Address to the Indian National Congress. In *Sources of Indian Tradition*, vol. 2. 2nd edition. Ed. Stephen Hay. New York: Columbia University Press, pp. 237–41

Bamford, P. C. [1925] 1974. *Histories of the Non-Co-operation and Khilafat Movements*. Delhi: Deep Publications. Reprint of Delhi: Government of India Press

Cannadine, David. 2001. *Ornamentalism: How the British Saw their Empire.* New York: Oxford University Press

Chander, Sunil. 1987. "Congress–Raj Conflict and the Rise of the Muslim League in the Ministry Period, 1937–39." In *Modern Asian Studies* 21, 2, pp. 303–328

Daechsel, Markus. 2006. *The Politics of Self-Expression: the Middle Class Milieu of Early 20th Century India and Pakistan.* New York: Routledge

Darul Uloom Deoband. 2007 [accessed]. http://www.darululoom-deoband.com/english/introulema/principals2.htm

Friedmann, Yohanan. 1971. "The Attitude of the *Jami'yyat-i 'Ulama'-i Hind* to the Indian National Movement and the Establishment of Pakistan." In *The 'Ulama' in Modern History. Asian and African Studies*, VII. Jerusalem: Israel Oriental Society, pp. 157–180

Friedmann, Yohanan. 1976. "The *Jami'yyat-i Ulama-i-Hind* in the Wake of Partition." In *Asian and African Studies* 11, 2, pp. 181–211

Fromkin, David. 1990. *A Peace to End All Peace: The Fall of the Ottoman Empire and the Creation of the Modern Middle East.* New York: Avon Books

Ghosh, Papiya. 1997. "Muttahidah Qaumiyat in Aqalliat Bihar: The Imarat-i-Shariah, 1921–1947." In *Indian Economic and Social History Review* 34, 1, pp. 1–20

Gilmartin, David. 2005. "A Networked Civilization?" In *Muslim Networks: From Hajj to Hip Hop*. Chapel Hill: University of North Carolina Press, pp. 51–68

Gooptu, Nandini. 2001. *The Politics of the Urban Poor in Early Twentieth-Century India*. Cambridge: Cambridge University Press

Goswami, Manu. 2004. *Producing India: From Colonial Economy to National Space*. Chicago: University of Chicago Press

Hardy, Peter. 1971. *Partners in Freedom and True Muslims: The Political Thought of Some Muslim Scholars in British India, 1912–47*. Lund, Studientliteratur

Hasan, Mushirul. 1998. "Traditional Rites and Contested Meanings: Sectarian Strife in Colonial Lucknow." In *Islam, Communities and the Nation: Muslim Identities in South Asia and Beyond*. Ed. Mushirul Hasan. Delhi: Manohar, pp. 341–366

Hasan, Mushirul and Margrit Pernau, eds. 2005. *Regionalizing Pan-Islamism: Documents on the Khilafat Movement*. New Delhi: Manohar

Hunter, W. W. 1871. *The Indian Musalmans: Are They Bound in Conscience to Rebel against the Queen?* London: Trubner & Co.

Iqbal, Muhammad. *Speeches and Statements of Iqbal*. 1973. Compiled by A. R. Tariq. Lahore: Sh. Ghulam Ali & Sons

Jalal, Ayesha. 1995. *The Sole Spokesman: Jinnah, the Muslim League, and the Demand for Pakistan*. Cambridge: Cambridge University Press

Mamdani, Mahmood. 2004. *Good Muslim, Bad Muslim: America, the Cold War, and the Roots of Terror*. New York: Pantheon

Manglori, Tufail Ahmad. 1994. *Towards a Common Destiny: A Nationalist Manifesto*. Translation of *Musalmanon ka Raushan Mustaqbil*. Trans. Ali Ashraf. New Delhi: People's Publishing House

Mayaram, Shaila. 1997. *Resisting Regimes: Myth, Memory and the Shaping of a Muslim Identity*. Delhi: Oxford University Press

Metcalf, Barbara. 1993. "Living Hadith in the Tablighi Jama'at." *The Journal of Asian Studies* 52, 3, pp. 584–608

Metcalf, Barbara. 2002. *Islamic Revival in British India: Deoband 1860–1900*. 2nd edition. New Delhi: Oxford University Press

Metcalf, Barbara. 2002b. "'Traditionalist' Islamic Activism: Deoband, Tablighis, and Talibs." In *Understanding September 11*. Ed. Craig Calhoun, Paul Price and Ashley Timmers. New York: The New Press, pp. 53–66

Metcalf, Barbara. 2004. "The Past in the Present: Instruction, Pleasure, and Blessing in Maulana Muhammad Zakariyya's *Aap Biitii*." In *Telling Lives in*

India: Biography, Autobiography, and Life History. Ed. David Arnold and Stuart Blackburn. New Delhi: Permanent Black, pp. 116–143

Metcalf, Barbara. 2005. "Iqbal's Imagined Geographies: The East, the West, the Nation, and Islam." In *A Wilderness of Possibilities: Urdu Studies in Transnational Perspective*. Ed. Kathryn Hansen and David Lelyveld. New York: Columbia University Press, and New Delhi: Oxford University Press

Metcalf, Barbara D. and Thomas R. Metcalf. 2006. *A Concise History of Modern India*. 2nd edition. Cambridge: Cambridge University Press

Minault, Gail. 1982. *The Khilafat Movement: Religious Symbolism and Political Mobilization in India*. Delhi: Oxford University Press

Muhammad Zakariyya Kandhlawi. [1928–1929] 2004. *The Differences of the Imams*. Trans. Mawlana Muhammad Kadwa. Santa Barbara: White Thread Press

Muhammad Zakariyya. [1938] 1994. *Al-Eti'daal fe Maraatibur-Rijaal* ("Islamic Politics"). New Delhi: Idara isha'at-e-diniyat

Muhammad Zakariyya Kandhlawi. 1971. *Aap biitii nambar 5 yaa yaad-i ayaam nambar 6*. Saharanpur: Kutbkhaana Yahyawii

Nevill, H. R. 1905. *Fyzabad: A Gazetteer being Volume XLIII of the District Gazetteers of the United Provinces of Agra and Oudh*. Allahabad: Government Press, United Provinces

Pandey, Gyanendra. 2001. *Remembering Partition: Violence, Nationalism, and History in India*. Cambridge: Cambridge University Press

Pirzada, A. S. Sayyid. 2000. *The Politics of the Jamiat Ulema-i-Islam Pakistan, 1971–77*. Karachi: Oxford University Press

Rizvi, Sayyid Mahboob. 1980. *History of the Dar al-Ulum Deoband*, vol. 1. Trans. Murtaz Husain F. Quraishi. Deoband: Idara-e Ihtemam, Dar al-Ulum Deoband

Roy, Asim. 1990. "The High Politics of India's Partition: The Revisionist Perspective." In *Modern Asian Studies* 24, 2, pp. 385–415

Roy, Olivier. 1994. *The Failure of Political Islam*. Cambridge: Harvard University Press.

Sanyal, Usha. 1996. *Devotional Islam and Politics in British India: Ahmad Riza Khan Barelwi and his Movement, 1870–1920*. New York: Oxford University Press

Sanyal, Usha. 2006. *Ahmad Riza Khan Barelwi: In the Path of the Prophet*. Oxford: Oneworld

Savarkar, Vinayak Damodar. [1923] 1988. *Hindutva*. In *Sources of Indian Tradition*, vol. 2. 2nd edition. Ed. Stephen Hay. New York: Columbia University Press, pp. 289–295

Singha, Radhika. 1998. *A Despotism of Law: Crime and Justice in Early Colonial India*. Oxford: Oxford University Press

Sinha, Mrinalini. 2006. *Specters of Mother India: The Global Restructuring of an Empire*. Durham: Duke University Press

Thanvi, Maulana Ashraf 'Ali. 2004. "The *Raison d'être* of Madrasah" (*Du 'at al Ummah wa Hudat al Millah*). Trans. M. al-Ghazali. *Islamic Studies* 43, 4, pp. 653–675

Zaman, Muhammad Qasim. 2002. *The Ulama in Contemporary Islam: Custodians of Change*. Princeton: Princeton University Press

Zaman, Muhammad Qasim. 2008. *Ashraf 'Ali Thanawi: Islam in Modern South Asia*. Oxford: Oneworld

INDEX

Madani, Husain Ahmad (*cont.*):
  Court of Sessions trial 84–5
  courts arrest 104–5
  daily routine 127
  Dars-i Qur'an ki sat majlis 127
  at Deoband 20–1, 57–62
  dreams 28–9, 60, 61–2, 63, 64,
    88–9
  effects of prison life on 41–3
  family 41–2, 51–4
  greater *jihad* 151
  identified as Deobandi 155
  imprisonment 56–7, 85, 139
  interrogations 37–40
  letters 100–1
  Malta, prison experience 35–40
  Malta, journey to 32–4
  marriages 68–9, 88, 124
  moves to the Hijaz 61–2
  Mujahid-i Jalil 126–7
  Muttahida Qaumiyyat aur Islam 112–17
  names 9–10
  Naqsh-i hayat 127, 133
  organization of volunteers 90
  "Our India and its Virtues" 131, 134
  Padma Vibhusan award 153
  principal of Deoband 92–3
  The Prisoner of Malta 13
  relationships 99–100
  released from prison 48–9
  as *sayyid* 51–2
  scholarly projects 46
  in Sylhet 88–92
  teaching 106, 107
  tribunal 30–2
  visits Pakistan 153–5
madh-i sahaba 122
Madina (journal) 130
Madrasa 'Aliya, Calcutta 87, 88
Mahmud Ahmad 41, 57, 61
Majid, Khwaja Abdul 143
Majlis-i-Ahrar 102, 141
Malaviya, Madan Mohan 77
Malta
  camp layout 35–6
  conditions 37
  interrogations 37–40
Mamdani, Mahmood 3
Manglori, Tufail Ahmad 130

marriage 94
  expenditure of 90–1
Mashriqi, 'Inayatullah 97, 119
Maududi, Abul A'la 97, 119–20, 122,
    135–8
Mayaram, Shail 153
Mayo, Katherine 94
Mewat 153
Mirza Ghulam Ahmad 66
Montagu-Chelmsford Reforms (1919)
    76, 94
Montagu Declaration (1917) 76
Mother India (Mayo) 94
Mountbatten, Lord 145
Muhammad Ahmad, Hafiz 20, 21, 88
Muhammad 'Ali 22, 32
  arrest of 82
  Ottoman cause 74
  president of Jamiat Ulama 102
  trial 83, 84
Muhammad Miyan 41, 87, 126–7
Muhammad, Prophet of Islam 62, 64,
    100, 114, 154
Muhammad Siddiq Ahmad 61, 63
Muhammad Zakariyya Kandhlawi 60,
    120–1, 146–8
Muinuddin Chisti 52
Mujaddid, Pir Ghulam 82, 83
Mujahid-i Jalil (Madani) 126–7
Musalmanon ka raushan mustaqbil (Manglori)
    130
Muslim Brotherhood 136
Muslim League 76, 101
  1936 elections 110–11
  and the Jamiat Ulama-i-Hind 141–3
  Lahore Resolution 128
  at Lucknow 123
  meeting at Simla 140
  as mouthpiece for Indian Muslims 112
  Second World War 124
Muslim League Parliamentary Board
    110–11
Muslim Parliamentary Board 141
Muslims
  British policy concerning 19
  fighting Muslims 81–2
  geographic autonomy 112
  identity and Partition 153
  India as ancestral home 132